Loving Someone with Quiet BPD

A Partner's Guide

Mason Ronald Goldstein

This book is for educational and informational purposes only and is not intended as a substitute for professional medical, psychological, or psychiatric advice, diagnosis, or treatment. The information contained herein is based on research, clinical observations, and the experiences of individuals in relationships with people who have borderline personality disorder presentations.

All success stories and case studies presented in this book are composite narratives created from patterns observed across multiple forum discussions, online support communities, and published experiences. These composite stories are designed to illustrate common relationship dynamics and do not represent any actual persons, living or deceased. Any resemblance to specific individuals is purely coincidental.

The names and identifying details used in all examples have been created specifically for illustrative purposes and do not refer to real people or situations.

While this book focuses on quiet or internalized presentations of borderline personality disorder, every individual's experience is unique. Professional consultation with qualified mental health providers is strongly recommended for diagnosis, treatment planning, and crisis intervention.

The strategies and approaches discussed in this book are not guaranteed to resolve relationship difficulties or improve outcomes in all situations. Readers are encouraged to use their judgment and seek professional guidance when implementing any techniques or making decisions about their relationships.

.

Table of Contents

Chapter 1: When Love Feels Like a Ghost Story

You know something's wrong, but you can't put your finger on what it is. Your partner seems wonderful to everyone else - supportive, caring, present. Yet you find yourself walking on eggshells around feelings you can't name, managing emotions that seem to shift like shadows. You question your own perceptions daily. Friends tell you how lucky you are, and you wonder why you feel so alone in what should be a loving relationship.

This disconnect between appearance and reality isn't in your head. What you're experiencing has a name: the invisible emotional world of quiet borderline personality disorder (BPD). Unlike the dramatic presentations most people associate with BPD, quiet BPD turns all that emotional chaos inward, creating a relationship dynamic that feels like loving a ghost - someone who's physically present but emotionally unreachable in ways you can't quite explain.

The Perfect Partner Illusion

Here's what makes quiet BPD so confusing for partners: the person you love has learned to manage their emotional storms by hiding them completely. They've developed what we might call a "perfect partner" facade - a carefully maintained presentation that everything is fine, they're handling things well, and any relationship problems must be coming from somewhere else.

This isn't manipulation in the traditional sense. It's more like emotional camouflage that developed as a survival mechanism. The person with quiet BPD learned early that showing emotional distress led to rejection or criticism, so they went underground with their feelings. They became experts at appearing stable while drowning internally.

You might notice patterns like these:

- Your partner handles stress with an almost unnatural calm
- They rarely ask for emotional support, even during difficult times
- When you try to discuss relationship concerns, they seem genuinely puzzled
- They take responsibility for everything while somehow making you feel like you're the problem
- Others consistently praise your partner's emotional maturity and stability

The challenge is that this perfect presentation comes at a cost - not just for them, but for the relationship itself. When someone consistently hides their authentic emotional experience, true intimacy becomes impossible. You're essentially in a relationship with a performance rather than a person.

How Quiet BPD Differs from What You Know

Most people's understanding of BPD comes from dramatic portrayals of explosive emotions, relationship chaos, and visible crisis. Quiet BPD flips this script entirely. Instead of external emotional storms, everything happens internally. Instead of obvious relationship drama, there's a subtle but persistent emotional disconnect that leaves partners feeling confused and gasping for air.

Classic BPD behaviors you won't see:

- Angry outbursts or emotional explosions
- Dramatic relationship conflicts or ultimatums
- Visible self-destructive behaviors

- Obvious patterns of idealization and devaluation

- Clear abandonment panic or clingy behavior

Quiet BPD patterns you might recognize:

- Emotional withdrawal that comes out of nowhere

- Taking criticism (even gentle feedback) extremely personally while appearing calm

- Perfectionism that seems to mask deep insecurity

- Difficulty accessing or expressing authentic emotions

- A tendency to disappear emotionally during conflict

The invisibility of these patterns is exactly what makes them so challenging for partners. You're dealing with the same core emotional dysregulation that drives all BPD presentations, but it's been pushed so far underground that even the person experiencing it might not recognize what's happening.

Why Traditional Help Falls Short

If you've tried to find support for your relationship struggles, you've probably discovered that most BPD resources don't fit your experience. Books about "walking on eggshells" assume visible emotional volatility. Support groups focus on managing dramatic behaviors that simply don't exist in your relationship.

This creates a secondary problem: you start to doubt whether your concerns are valid. After all, your partner isn't throwing things or threatening self-harm. They're not cycling through extreme emotions or creating obvious chaos. From the outside, everything looks fine. Maybe the problem really is you.

But here's what traditional BPD resources miss: the absence of external drama doesn't mean the absence of emotional dysfunction. In fact, quiet BPD can be even more challenging for relationships because the problems are harder to identify and address. You're dealing with:

- **Emotional unavailability disguised as stability**

- **Conflict avoidance that prevents real resolution**

- **Perfectionism that creates unrealistic relationship standards**

- **Internal self-criticism that leaks into the relationship in subtle ways**

- **Attachment fears that manifest as emotional distance rather than clingy behavior**

The Gaslighting Effect of Invisible Symptoms

One of the most challenging aspects of being in a relationship with someone who has quiet BPD is what we might call "reality distortion." This isn't intentional gaslighting where someone deliberately makes you question your perceptions. Instead, it's the natural result of being with someone whose emotional reality is completely hidden.

You develop almost supernatural sensitivity to emotional atmospheres because you're constantly trying to read invisible cues. You notice tension that your partner denies exists. You sense distance that they don't acknowledge. You feel responsible for emotional dynamics that seem to have no source.

Over time, this creates a pattern where you:

- Question your emotional intelligence

- Doubt your relationship instincts

- Take responsibility for problems you can't identify

- Feel "crazy" for sensing issues that seem to have no basis

- Become hypervigilant about your partner's moods and needs

4

The effect is particularly pronounced because people with quiet BPD often have highly developed emotional radar themselves. They can be incredibly attuned to your emotional state while remaining completely disconnected from their own. This creates an unbalanced dynamic where you're both managing your emotions and theirs, often without even realizing it.

Recognizing the Hidden Patterns

Is Your Partner's Emotional Experience Internalized?

Consider these questions honestly:

Emotional Expression:

- Does your partner rarely show strong emotions, even during stressful situations?

- Do they seem uncomfortable when you express emotions freely?

- Have you noticed them minimizing their own feelings or experiences?

- Do they appear unusually calm during times that would typically cause stress?

Communication Patterns:

- Does your partner avoid deep emotional conversations?

- Do they change the subject when discussions become too personal?

- Do you find yourself doing most of the emotional work in the relationship?

- Does your partner seem confused when you express relationship concerns?

Relationship Dynamics:

- Do you feel like you're walking on invisible eggshells?

- Do you find yourself constantly monitoring your partner's mood?

- Does your partner seem to need frequent reassurance while denying they need support?

- Do you feel emotionally exhausted without obvious reasons?

Self-Perception:

- Do you question your own emotional instincts more than you used to?

- Have you started doubting whether your relationship concerns are valid?

- Do you feel responsible for problems you can't clearly identify?

- Does your partner seem perfect to others while you experience private stress?

If you're recognizing several of these patterns, you're not losing your mind. You're accurately perceiving the effects of internalized emotional dysregulation on your relationship.

Validating Your Experience

Your perceptions are valid. The confusion you feel makes perfect sense. You're not being oversensitive, demanding, or difficult. You're responding naturally to an unnatural emotional situation.

Living with someone who experiences intense emotions while showing none of them creates a unique form of relationship stress. You're picking up on emotional undercurrents that exist but remain unacknowledged. You're trying to connect with someone who desperately wants connection but has learned that emotional vulnerability equals danger.

Simple validation exercises:

Daily emotional check-ins: Trust your instincts about the emotional atmosphere in your home. If something feels off, it probably is - even if there's no obvious explanation.

Pattern documentation: Notice when you feel confused or frustrated in your relationship. These moments often point to invisible emotional dynamics that deserve attention.

Self-compassion practice: Remind yourself that confusion is the natural response to mixed emotional signals. You're not failing as a partner; you're responding appropriately to a challenging situation.

A Real-World Example

Consider a working professional whose partner sought individual therapy for relationship anxiety. The professional appeared emotionally stable, career-focused, and committed to their relationship. Friends and family consistently praised their maturity and supportiveness.

However, their partner described feeling constantly on edge without understanding why. They reported walking on invisible eggshells, managing emotional atmospheres they couldn't explain, and questioning their own relationship instincts daily. The professional genuinely seemed confused by these concerns and suggested their partner might benefit from anxiety medication.

What became clear through careful observation was that the professional managed emotions through rigid internal control. They experienced intense fear around criticism, rejection, and conflict but expressed none of these fears externally. Instead, they withdrew emotionally whenever these triggers arose, creating distance their partner could feel but couldn't identify.

The professional took responsibility for all relationship problems while simultaneously avoiding any conversation that might reveal their emotional vulnerability. They maintained perfect partner status by never allowing their authentic emotional experience to surface. This created a relationship dynamic where their partner felt simultaneously loved and utterly alone.

The breakthrough came when the professional recognized that their emotional self-protection was actually creating the very abandonment they feared. Their partner wasn't leaving because of emotional intensity - they were considering leaving because of emotional unavailability.

Breaking Through the Confusion

Understanding quiet BPD doesn't solve everything overnight, but it provides the missing piece of the relationship puzzle. When you realize that your partner's emotional storms are happening internally rather than externally, their behavior starts making sense in a completely different way.

That sudden emotional distance? It might follow something they perceived as criticism. That perfect calm during stressful situations? It could be emotional shutdown rather than emotional stability. That confusion when you express relationship concerns? They might genuinely not recognize their own contribution to the problems because their emotional experience remains unconscious.

What this means for you:

- Your relationship instincts are probably more accurate than you realize

- The emotional work you're doing matters, even if it goes unrecognized

- Your confusion points to real relationship dynamics that need attention

- You're not responsible for fixing or managing your partner's emotional experience

- Change is possible, but it requires recognition and commitment from both people

The Path to Clarity

Recognizing quiet BPD in your relationship isn't about assigning blame or creating excuses. It's about understanding the invisible dynamics that have been shaping your experience so you can respond more effectively.

When emotional storms happen internally, traditional relationship tools often fall short. You can't resolve conflicts that never surface. You can't support someone who won't acknowledge they need support. You can't build intimacy with someone who's afraid to be emotionally vulnerable.

But you can learn to recognize the signs of internal emotional distress. You can develop communication strategies that feel safe for someone who fears emotional expression. You can protect your own emotional well-being while still offering genuine support.

Most importantly, you can trust your perceptions again. The relationship dynamics you've been sensing are real, even if they've been invisible. Your emotional exhaustion makes sense. Your confusion is completely understandable. You haven't been imagining problems or creating drama where none exists.

What Becomes Possible

Relationships involving quiet BPD can absolutely thrive with the right understanding and approach. When both people recognize what's actually happening emotionally, real intimacy becomes possible for the first time.

The person with quiet BPD can learn that emotional vulnerability doesn't automatically lead to rejection. They can discover that authentic connection feels better than perfect performance. They can experience the relief of being loved for who they really are rather than who they think they need to be.

Partners can stop walking on invisible eggshells and start addressing real relationship dynamics. They can rebuild trust in their emotional instincts while learning to distinguish between their own feelings and their partner's hidden emotional experience.

The ghost story can transform into a genuine love story - but only with recognition, understanding, and commitment to emotional authenticity from both people involved.

Armed with this understanding, you're ready to explore exactly how quiet BPD manifests in relationships and what you can do to create the genuine connection you've been seeking. The invisible is about to become visible, and that changes everything.

Chapter 2: The Silent Language of Internalized Pain

Imagine trying to learn a foreign language where the speaker never opens their mouth. You sense meaning behind their expressions, notice subtle changes in their posture, feel the emotional undercurrents of what they're not saying. This is what it's like living with someone who has quiet BPD - you're constantly trying to decode a silent language of internalized pain that operates below the surface of everyday interaction.

Unlike the dramatic emotional displays most people associate with BPD, quiet BPD speaks in whispers. Emotional storms happen entirely internally. Crisis moments look like calm withdrawal. The intense fear of abandonment gets expressed through emotional distance rather than clingy behavior. For partners, this creates a unique challenge: how do you respond to pain you can't see and support someone who's determined to handle everything alone?

The key lies in understanding that the same emotional intensity exists - it's just been redirected inward. Learning to recognize this silent language isn't about becoming a mind reader; it's about developing awareness of the subtle ways deep emotional pain expresses itself when someone has learned that showing feelings equals danger.

The Overcontrol Phenomenon

Dr. Thomas Lynch's groundbreaking work revealed something fascinating about certain personality types: some people develop what's called "overcontrol" as their primary way of managing emotions. Instead of emotions flowing naturally, everything gets tightly regulated, suppressed, and managed through rigid internal systems.

Think of it like an internal pressure cooker. On the outside, everything appears calm and controlled. Inside, intense emotions build up pressure with no safe outlet. The person becomes an expert at containing their emotional experience while losing the ability to express, process, or even fully recognize what they're feeling.

Four core areas where overcontrol shows up:

1. **Emotional expression**: They struggle to show feelings appropriately, often appearing too calm during stressful situations or completely shutdown during emotional moments

2. **Interpersonal connections**: Despite desperately wanting close relationships, they maintain emotional walls that prevent genuine intimacy

3. **Flexible responding**: They have difficulty adapting when life doesn't go according to plan, often becoming rigid or withdrawn when faced with unexpected changes

4. **Social signaling**: They miss or ignore social cues about when emotional expression would be appropriate or helpful

For partners, this means you're in a relationship with someone who experiences intense emotions but has essentially locked them away. They want connection but fear vulnerability. They need support but can't ask for it. They experience pain but hide it so effectively that even they might not recognize it.

The Two-Self Split

People with quiet BPD often develop what feels like two distinct selves: the "normal self" that handles daily life and the "wounded self" that carries all the emotional pain. This isn't the same as multiple personality disorder - it's more like emotional compartmentalization taken to an extreme.

The normal self is who you see most of the time. This self goes to work, manages responsibilities, maintains friendships, and appears emotionally stable. The normal self genuinely wants to be a good partner and often succeeds at meeting external expectations.

The wounded self carries all the BPD symptoms: the abandonment fears, the emotional instability, the identity confusion, the intense shame. But this self remains hidden, sometimes even from the person experiencing it. The wounded self might emerge briefly during private moments - through self-critical thoughts, secret emotional breakdowns, or internal self-harm behaviors - but quickly gets pushed back down.

How this affects relationships:

- You feel like you're dating two different people, but only one is allowed to exist publicly

- Your partner might seem genuinely confused when you point out emotional patterns

- Intimate conversations feel surface-level because the wounded self can't safely appear

- You sense emotional depth that never quite becomes accessible

- Your partner takes responsibility for relationship problems while the wounded self remains convinced they're fundamentally flawed

The challenge for partners is that you often sense the wounded self's presence without ever getting to interact with it directly. You feel the emotional undercurrents, notice the subtle signs of internal struggle, but the normal self insists everything is fine.

Hidden Crisis Indicators

When someone internalizes their emotional experience, crisis moments don't look like what you'd expect. There's no dramatic breakdown, no obvious call for help, no visible signs of distress.

Instead, you learn to recognize subtle shifts that indicate internal emotional chaos.

Emotional shutdown signals:

- Suddenly becoming unusually quiet or withdrawn
- Responding to questions with minimal words or apparent confusion
- Appearing physically present but emotionally absent
- Developing a blank or distant expression during conversations
- Seeming to "go through the motions" of normal activities

Internal self-harm indicators:

- Increased self-critical comments that seem disproportionate
- Mentioning feeling "numb" or "empty" in passing
- Sudden changes in sleep or eating patterns
- Withdrawing from physical affection or intimate connection
- Expressing feeling like a "burden" or that others would be "better off without them"

Dissociation signs:

- Seeming confused about time or recent events
- Appearing "spacey" or having difficulty concentrating
- Responding with unusual delay to questions or interactions
- Mentioning feeling "unreal" or like they're "watching themselves"
- Having difficulty remembering conversations or commitments

The tricky part is that these signs often get dismissed as tiredness, stress, or normal mood variation. Your partner might even dismiss them themselves, attributing internal crisis to external factors like work pressure or being busy.

The Attachment Paradox

Here's one of the most confusing aspects of quiet BPD: the person simultaneously craves close connection and fears it intensely. This creates what we might call an "attachment paradox" - they need emotional intimacy to feel secure but experience emotional intimacy as threatening.

How this shows up in relationships:

Approach-avoidance cycles: Your partner seeks closeness and connection, then pulls away when things feel too intimate or vulnerable. This isn't game-playing; it's the result of conflicting internal systems.

Emotional labor imbalance: They want you to be emotionally available and expressive while maintaining strict control over their own emotional expression. You end up doing the emotional work for both people.

Criticism sensitivity: Even gentle feedback feels like rejection or abandonment to someone with BPD, but quiet BPD means this reaction gets internalized rather than expressed. You might notice withdrawal or shutdown rather than defensive anger.

Independence versus connection: They maintain fierce independence as protection against abandonment while secretly longing for someone to truly see and understand their internal experience.

The attachment paradox explains why relationships with quiet BPD can feel simultaneously intimate and distant. Your partner wants the connection you're offering but can't risk the vulnerability it requires.

Recognizing Distress Signals

The Emotional Thermometer

Since traditional emotional expression is limited, you need to develop sensitivity to more subtle indicators of your partner's internal temperature.

Physical indicators:

- Changes in posture or energy level
- Tension in shoulders, jaw, or facial expressions
- Shifts in breathing patterns during conversations
- Unusual restlessness or stillness
- Changes in eye contact or facial expressiveness

Behavioral indicators:

- Increased perfectionism or control over environment
- Changes in routine or normal habits
- Withdrawal from activities they usually enjoy
- Increased focus on work or external responsibilities
- Changes in communication patterns (shorter responses, delayed replies)

Emotional atmosphere indicators:

- The room feeling heavier or more tense without obvious reason
- Sensing distance even when physically close
- Feeling like you're walking on invisible barriers
- Noticing your own anxiety or vigilance increase around your partner

- Experiencing the urge to be extra careful with your words or actions

Communication Behind the Wall

People with quiet BPD often communicate indirectly because direct emotional expression feels too vulnerable. Learning to decode these indirect communications can help you respond more effectively to their actual needs.

Translation guide for indirect expressions:

"I'm fine" might mean: "I'm struggling but can't risk being vulnerable right now"

"I don't want to bother you" often means: "I desperately need support but feel like a burden"

"It's not a big deal" usually translates to: "This is huge for me but I'm minimizing to stay safe"

"I'm just tired" can mean: "I'm emotionally overwhelmed but don't have words for it"

"I need some space" might indicate: "I'm having intense emotions and need to regulate privately"

"You deserve better" often means: "I'm convinced I'm fundamentally flawed and will hurt you"

The key is learning to hear the emotional need behind the words rather than taking the surface message at face value. This doesn't mean ignoring what they say, but rather understanding that someone with quiet BPD has learned to express needs in ways that feel emotionally safe.

A Real-World Learning Story

Consider a software engineer whose partner began noticing subtle patterns over time. The engineer maintained excellent work performance, managed household responsibilities efficiently, and seemed emotionally stable to friends and family. However, their partner observed recurring cycles that seemed to have no external trigger.

The pattern looked like this: The engineer would become unusually quiet for several days, responding to questions with minimal words while maintaining normal daily routines. During these periods, they'd work longer hours, organize areas of the house that were already clean, and decline social invitations without explanation.

Initially, the partner attributed these cycles to work stress or natural introversion. But careful observation revealed the pattern often followed situations involving criticism, conflict (even minor disagreements), or expressions of emotional need from others.

The breakthrough came when the partner learned to recognize these quiet periods as emotional crisis rather than simple withdrawal. Instead of trying to draw the engineer out through direct questions, they began offering subtle support: preparing favorite meals, handling extra household tasks, and providing gentle physical affection without demanding emotional reciprocation.

The engineer eventually revealed that these periods involved intense internal self-criticism, overwhelming shame, and urges to withdraw from the relationship entirely. They experienced each perceived mistake or moment of conflict as evidence of their fundamental inadequacy as a partner. The quiet periods represented internal emotional breakdown that they managed through rigid control and isolation.

Understanding this pattern allowed both people to develop better ways of handling these cycles. The engineer learned to recognize early warning signs of emotional spiral and communicate needs more directly. The partner learned to provide support without taking the withdrawal personally and to distinguish between normal alone time and crisis-related shutdown.

Building Your Decoder Skills

Daily observation practice: Start noticing the subtle emotional atmosphere in your relationship without trying to fix or change anything. Simply become aware of when things feel different, even if you can't identify why.

Pattern tracking: Keep notes about your partner's emotional rhythm over several weeks. What precedes periods of withdrawal? What seems to help during difficult times? What patterns emerge?

Indirect communication recognition: Practice listening for the emotional need behind indirect communications. When your partner minimizes something, ask yourself what they might actually be experiencing internally.

Your own emotional thermometer: Notice your own anxiety, confusion, or hypervigilance as potential indicators of your partner's internal distress. Your emotional system often picks up on things before your logical mind does.

The Internal Self-Harm Reality

One of the most concerning aspects of quiet BPD is that self-destructive behaviors often remain completely internal and invisible. While classic BPD might involve visible self-harm, quiet BPD channels these impulses into internal self-attack that can be equally damaging.

Forms of internal self-harm:

- Relentless self-criticism and negative self-talk
- Emotional punishment through isolation and withdrawal
- Denial of basic emotional needs and self-care
- Perfectionism that creates impossible standards
- Taking responsibility for things outside their control

How partners can recognize internal self-harm:

- Notice when your partner seems unusually hard on themselves

- Pay attention to self-deprecating comments that seem excessive

- Observe patterns of self-denial or refusing help

- Watch for perfectionism that creates stress rather than satisfaction

- Notice when they take blame for things that aren't their fault

Supporting someone through internal self-harm requires delicate balance. You can't force them to stop the internal attack, but you can offer consistent external validation and refuse to participate in the self-criticism.

Creating Safety for Authentic Expression

The goal isn't to force emotional expression but to create conditions where authentic feelings can safely emerge over time. This requires patience, consistency, and understanding that emotional walls developed over years won't come down overnight.

Practical approaches:

Validate without pushing: Acknowledge that your partner might be experiencing more than they're expressing without demanding they share more than feels safe.

Model emotional authenticity: Share your own feelings appropriately without making your partner responsible for managing them.

Respond to indirect communications: When your partner hints at needs indirectly, try responding to the underlying emotional message rather than just the surface words.

Create low-pressure opportunities: Offer support in ways that don't require vulnerability - preparing meals during stressful times, handling extra responsibilities, or simply being physically present.

Avoid emotional pursuing: When your partner withdraws, resist the urge to chase them emotionally. Instead, maintain steady, consistent availability without pressure.

The Long View of Change

Understanding quiet BPD doesn't lead to overnight transformation, but it does provide the missing piece for building genuine intimacy over time. When both people understand what's actually happening emotionally, real progress becomes possible.

Your partner can begin to recognize their internal emotional experience as valid rather than shameful. They can learn that emotional vulnerability doesn't automatically lead to rejection. Most importantly, they can discover that authentic connection feels better than perfect performance.

You can stop walking on invisible eggshells and start responding to actual relationship dynamics. You can rebuild trust in your emotional instincts while learning to distinguish between your feelings and your partner's hidden emotional experience.

The silent language of internalized pain doesn't have to remain silent forever. With understanding, patience, and the right approach, it can gradually become a shared language of genuine emotional connection.

Building upon these insights, you're ready to explore why living with quiet BPD can feel like walking on invisible eggshells - and what you can do to find solid ground in your relationship again.

Chapter 3: Walking on Invisible Eggshells

You've developed a sixth sense about your partner's moods that you never needed before. You find yourself analyzing their tone of voice, scanning their facial expressions for micro-changes, and adjusting your own behavior based on subtle shifts in the emotional atmosphere that others can't even detect. You're living in a state of constant low-level alertness, like a detective trying to solve a mystery where all the clues are hidden.

This hypervigilance isn't paranoia - it's a natural adaptation to living with someone whose emotional storms happen entirely internally. When there are no external warning signs of distress, you learn to read the invisible signals. When conflict gets buried rather than expressed, you become an expert at sensing underground tension. When your partner's emotional needs remain unspoken, you develop almost supernatural sensitivity to unspoken messages.

The exhausting reality is that you're walking on eggshells you can't see, avoiding triggers you can't identify, and managing emotional dynamics that officially don't exist. This creates its own unique form of relationship stress that feels both very real and completely invisible to the outside world.

The Invisible Trigger Map

In relationships with classic BPD, triggers are often obvious: raised voices, criticism, threats of abandonment, or changes in routine. With quiet BPD, triggers operate like hidden landmines. You step on them without knowing they exist and experience the aftermath without understanding what happened.

Common invisible triggers include:

Perceived criticism disguised as neutral feedback: Something as simple as "Hey, would you mind loading the dishwasher differently?" can trigger intense internal shame and abandonment fears, even though the request seems completely reasonable.

Success or positive attention: Ironically, good things happening can trigger internal crisis because they don't match your partner's self-concept or create fear that good things will be taken away.

Emotional intimacy moments: The very connection your partner craves can trigger panic about vulnerability and potential rejection, leading to sudden emotional withdrawal.

Changes in routine or plans: Even positive changes can feel threatening to someone who uses rigid control to manage internal emotional chaos.

Others' emotional needs: When you express your own emotional needs, it can trigger intense guilt and inadequacy in your partner, leading them to shut down rather than respond supportively.

The challenge is that these triggers often seem random or disproportionate to external observers. You might have a lovely evening together, share an intimate moment, and then find your partner emotionally unavailable for days afterward - with no apparent connection between the positive experience and the withdrawal.

The Hypervigilance Trap

Living with invisible triggers creates a psychological state called hypervigilance - a constant state of alertness where you're scanning for potential emotional threats. This isn't a conscious choice; it's your nervous system's adaptation to an unpredictable emotional environment.

How hypervigilance develops:

You start noticing that certain interactions precede your partner's emotional withdrawal. Maybe compliments seem to create distance.

Perhaps bringing up future plans leads to shutdown. Maybe expressions of love trigger anxiety rather than warmth.

Without understanding quiet BPD, you begin attributing these patterns to your own behavior. You become careful about giving compliments that might overwhelm. You avoid bringing up topics that seem to create tension. You learn to manage your partner's emotional experience by managing your own behavior.

Over time, this creates a relationship dynamic where you're constantly monitoring and adjusting. You develop an internal early warning system that's always running in the background, analyzing whether it's safe to express needs, share feelings, or even be authentically yourself.

Signs you've developed hypervigilance:

- You find yourself overthinking normal conversations

- You hesitate before expressing opinions or feelings

- You notice changes in your partner's mood before they do

- You feel responsible for managing the emotional atmosphere

- You're exhausted by the mental effort of constant monitoring

The cruel irony is that hypervigilance often makes things worse. The more you try to avoid triggers, the more walking-on-eggshells energy you bring to the relationship, which can actually trigger your partner's abandonment fears.

The Energy of Monitoring Internal Storms

Here's what people don't understand about quiet BPD relationships: the absence of external drama doesn't mean the absence of emotional intensity. It just means all that intensity gets channeled internally, and you become responsible for sensing and responding to storms you can't see.

Think about the energy it takes to be a weather forecaster for invisible weather systems. You're constantly reading atmospheric pressure, noticing subtle shifts in emotional climate, and preparing for storms that might hit without warning. You develop an exhausting expertise in emotional meteorology that you never wanted and that serves no purpose outside this specific relationship.

The hidden workload includes:

Emotional translation services: Converting indirect communications into actual needs ("I'm fine" = "I'm struggling but can't say so")

Mood management without acknowledgment: Adjusting your own energy and behavior based on your partner's internal emotional state while pretending you're not doing this

Crisis prevention through mind-reading: Trying to avoid triggers you can't identify through careful management of your own authenticity

Invisible emotional labor: Carrying the emotional weight for both people while your partner focuses on maintaining their controlled exterior

Validation without reciprocity: Providing constant emotional support while receiving little in return, because your partner can't acknowledge their need for support

This workload is particularly exhausting because it never gets recognized or appreciated. Your partner might genuinely believe they're low-maintenance and emotionally stable while you're quietly managing complex emotional dynamics behind the scenes.

Understanding Sudden Withdrawals

One of the most confusing aspects of quiet BPD relationships is the sudden emotional withdrawal that seems to come from nowhere. You're having a normal conversation, sharing a pleasant moment, or simply existing together when suddenly your partner becomes distant, cold, or unavailable.

These withdrawals aren't random - they're predictable responses to internal emotional triggers. The problem is that the triggers and the responses happen internally, leaving you to experience the effects without understanding the cause.

What sudden withdrawal might mean:

Shame spiral: Something triggered intense self-criticism or feelings of inadequacy, and your partner has withdrawn to manage these feelings privately.

Overwhelm response: Your partner reached their emotional capacity and needs to retreat to prevent total emotional dysregulation.

Abandonment panic: Ironically, moments of closeness can trigger fear of loss, leading to preemptive withdrawal as protection against potential rejection.

Identity confusion: Your partner is experiencing uncertainty about who they are or what they want and needs space to regulate internally.

Trigger recovery: Something activated their trauma response, and they're using isolation to self-soothe and regain emotional control.

The key insight is that withdrawal is often about internal emotional management rather than anything you did wrong. Your partner isn't punishing you; they're protecting themselves using the only emotional regulation tools they know how to use.

The Push-Pull Cycle

Quiet BPD creates a particular kind of relationship dance that feels like an endless cycle of approach and avoidance. Your partner wants closeness but fears vulnerability. They need support but can't ask for it. They love you but experience love as dangerous.

How the cycle typically works:

Connection phase: Things feel good between you. Your partner seems emotionally available and the relationship feels stable and loving.

Trigger phase: Something (often related to intimacy, success, or emotional expression) activates your partner's internal alarm system.

Withdrawal phase: Your partner becomes emotionally distant, physically absent, or generally unavailable without explanation.

Confusion phase: You try to understand what changed, often blaming yourself or wondering what you did wrong.

Pursuit phase: You might try to reconnect, fix the problem, or draw your partner back out, which often makes the withdrawal stronger.

Resolution phase: Eventually, your partner's internal emotional storm passes and they return to connection, often acting as if nothing happened.

This cycle is particularly crazy-making because it appears to be about the relationship when it's actually about your partner's internal emotional management. You're experiencing the side effects of their emotional regulation without access to the information that would help you understand what's really happening.

The HIDE Model

To help make sense of these invisible dynamics, here's a framework for understanding quiet BPD relationships:

H - Hidden emotions The person experiences intense emotions but keeps them completely internal. Anger becomes self-criticism. Sadness becomes numbness. Fear becomes control. You're in a relationship with someone's emotional performance rather than their emotional reality.

I - Internal struggles The real emotional battles happen entirely inside your partner's mind. They fight shame, manage abandonment fears, and regulate intense feelings without any external expression. You see the effects but never the actual struggle.

D - Disconnection patterns Your partner uses emotional distance as their primary regulation tool. Instead of expressing needs, they withdraw. Instead of processing conflict, they shut down. Instead of seeking support, they isolate.

E - Emotional exhaustion You become depleted from managing invisible emotional dynamics. You carry the emotional load for both people while your partner focuses on maintaining their controlled exterior. You're emotionally exhausted while your partner appears emotionally stable.

Understanding these four elements helps explain why quiet BPD relationships feel simultaneously intimate and distant, loving and confusing, stable and chaotic.

Mapping Your Own Invisible Triggers

Since you can't directly control your partner's triggers, focus on understanding your own patterns and responses. What situations tend to activate your hypervigilance? When do you start walking on invisible eggshells?

Common partner triggers:

- When your partner becomes unusually quiet
- After moments of emotional intimacy or connection
- When your partner seems "too perfect" or controlled
- During transitions or changes in routine
- When you sense tension that gets denied or minimized

Your own stress signals:

- Finding yourself overthinking normal interactions
- Feeling responsible for emotional atmospheres
- Hesitating to express authentic thoughts or feelings
- Noticing increased anxiety around your partner
- Feeling like you're performing in your own relationship

Recognizing these patterns helps you distinguish between appropriate relationship awareness and unhealthy hypervigilance. You want to be emotionally attuned to your partner without losing yourself in the process.

Practical Strategies for Invisible Dynamics

The emotional weather report: Instead of trying to fix or prevent your partner's emotional storms, practice simply noticing and naming what you observe: "I'm sensing some distance today" or "The energy feels different right now." This acknowledges reality without demanding explanation.

Boundary setting with kindness: You can support your partner's emotional regulation without taking responsibility for it. "I notice you seem stressed. I'm here if you want to talk, and I'm also going to take care of my own emotional needs."

The indirect response approach: When your partner communicates indirectly ("I'm fine" when they're clearly not), try responding to both levels: "I hear you saying you're fine, and I also sense you might be going through something. I'm here either way."

Maintaining your emotional center: Regular check-ins with yourself: "What am I feeling right now? What do I need? Am I taking responsibility for emotions that aren't mine?"

Creating connection without pursuit: Instead of chasing when your partner withdraws, try maintaining steady availability: "I'm not going anywhere. When you're ready to connect, I'll be here."

A Real-World Navigation Story

Consider a teacher whose partner was a successful marketing executive. The executive maintained excellent professional relationships, managed stress well, and appeared emotionally stable to everyone who knew them. However, the teacher noticed a pattern that seemed to have no external logic.

Every few weeks, usually after particularly good times together - successful work presentations, enjoyable social events, or intimate conversations - the executive would become distant and withdrawn. They'd work late, avoid physical affection, and respond to questions with minimal words. When asked directly, they'd insist nothing was wrong and seem genuinely confused by the teacher's concerns.

The teacher initially blamed themselves. Maybe they were being too needy after good times. Maybe they were imagining problems. Maybe they should just appreciate the good moments and not worry about the temporary distance.

But the pattern persisted, and the teacher began to feel like they were losing their mind. They started walking on invisible eggshells, being careful not to express too much joy after positive experiences, avoiding intimate conversations that might trigger withdrawal, and constantly monitoring the emotional atmosphere for signs of impending distance.

The breakthrough came when the teacher learned about quiet BPD and realized that positive experiences can trigger internal shame and abandonment fears. The executive wasn't withdrawing because anything was wrong; they were withdrawing because something felt too right, too good, too vulnerable.

Instead of pursuing during withdrawal periods, the teacher began responding differently. They'd continue their normal routines, maintain gentle availability, and avoid taking the distance personally. They'd say things like, "I'm here when you're ready" instead of "What's wrong?" or "Did I do something?"

Over time, the executive began to recognize their own pattern and eventually shared that good experiences triggered intense fear that "the other shoe would drop." They'd learned to protect themselves from disappointment by creating distance before connection could be taken away.

Understanding this pattern didn't eliminate it overnight, but it removed the confusion and blame that had been poisoning their relationship. The teacher stopped taking withdrawal personally, and the executive began to recognize their pattern as trauma response rather than relationship problem.

Breaking the Invisible Eggshell Pattern

The goal isn't to eliminate all emotional sensitivity or stop paying attention to your partner's internal experience. Healthy relationships require emotional attunement. The goal is to distinguish between appropriate awareness and unhealthy hypervigilance.

Healthy emotional awareness looks like:

- Noticing your partner's emotional state without feeling responsible for changing it

- Offering support without pursuing or demanding reciprocation

- Maintaining your own emotional center while staying open to connection

- Recognizing patterns without taking them personally

- Supporting your partner's growth without managing their emotions

Unhealthy hypervigilance looks like:

- Constantly monitoring and adjusting your behavior based on your partner's mood

- Feeling responsible for preventing or fixing your partner's emotional states

- Losing access to your own authentic emotions and needs

- Walking on eggshells around topics or expressions that might trigger withdrawal

- Exhausting yourself through emotional management that goes unrecognized

The Path Off Invisible Eggshells

Living with quiet BPD doesn't have to mean permanent hypervigilance and emotional exhaustion. When both people understand what's actually happening, the invisible can become visible and manageable.

Your partner can learn to recognize their internal emotional patterns and communicate more directly about their needs. They can discover that vulnerability doesn't automatically lead to abandonment and that authentic connection feels better than perfect control.

You can learn to distinguish between your emotions and your partner's, offering support without taking responsibility for emotional outcomes. You can rebuild trust in your own perceptions while maintaining appropriate boundaries around emotional labor.

The invisible eggshells can become visible relationship dynamics that both people can address consciously and collaboratively.

Most importantly, you can stop feeling crazy for sensing problems that officially don't exist. Your emotional instincts are picking up on real relationship dynamics that deserve attention and understanding, not dismissal or minimization.

These discoveries guide us toward practical communication strategies that honor both your need for emotional authenticity and your partner's need for emotional safety. When invisible dynamics become visible and manageable, real intimacy finally becomes possible.

Chapter 4: Speaking to Someone Who Can't Speak Their Truth

Communication in relationships typically relies on a basic assumption: both people can express their needs, feelings, and concerns directly. But what happens when one person has learned that emotional expression equals danger? What do you do when your partner experiences intense emotions but has no safe way to share them? How do you build intimacy with someone who's afraid to be vulnerable?

In quiet BPD relationships, traditional communication strategies often fall flat because they assume emotional availability that simply doesn't exist. Your partner isn't choosing to be indirect or mysterious - they've developed sophisticated emotional protection systems that make authentic expression feel impossible. The very conversations that could bring you closer together trigger their deepest fears of rejection and abandonment.

This creates a communication paradox: the more you try to get your partner to open up using conventional approaches, the more they're likely to shut down. The harder you pursue emotional connection, the more they'll retreat into protective silence. Yet underneath that silence lies a person desperately longing for understanding and connection.

Why Direct Communication Feels Dangerous

For someone with quiet BPD, sharing authentic emotions carries enormous perceived risk. Their emotional protection system developed early in life when expressing feelings led to criticism, dismissal, or rejection. Even though you're not the person who originally hurt them, their nervous system can't distinguish between past danger and present safety.

What makes emotional expression feel threatening:

Fear of being seen as "too much": Past experiences taught them that their emotional intensity overwhelms others, so they've learned to contain everything internally.

Perfectionism as protection: Maintaining a calm, controlled exterior feels safer than risking the vulnerability of authentic expression.

Shame about emotional needs: They believe their feelings are wrong, inappropriate, or burdensome, so sharing them feels like exposing fundamental inadequacy.

Terror of abandonment: If you really knew how they felt inside, you might realize they're not worth staying with (according to their internal belief system).

Loss of control fears: Emotional expression feels like opening floodgates they might not be able to close again.

Understanding these fears doesn't mean accepting poor communication forever, but it does mean approaching the problem differently. You can't force someone to feel safe - you can only create conditions where safety becomes possible over time.

Creating Emotional Safety Without Pressure

Traditional advice about improving communication usually involves encouraging more openness, asking direct questions about feelings, or expressing frustration when your partner won't share. With quiet BPD, these approaches often backfire because they increase pressure around the very thing that feels most dangerous.

Safety-building approaches:

Validate without pursuing: "I can see you're going through something. You don't have to tell me about it, but I want you to know I'm here."

Share your own feelings appropriately: Model emotional authenticity without making your partner responsible for reciprocating or managing your emotions.

Respond to actions rather than words: When your partner's behavior suggests distress, respond to what you observe rather than demanding verbal confirmation.

Create low-stakes emotional interactions: Share smaller feelings and observations that don't require deep vulnerability, giving your partner safe opportunities to practice emotional connection.

Respect their timeline: Emotional safety develops slowly. Pushing for faster progress often creates more fear and withdrawal.

The goal is to demonstrate through consistent actions that emotional expression won't lead to rejection, criticism, or demands for more than they can safely give.

The Art of Indirect Response

Since people with quiet BPD often communicate indirectly, learning to respond to the emotional message behind their words can be more effective than addressing only the surface content.

Translation skills for common indirect communications:

When they say "I'm fine" but seem withdrawn: Instead of challenging the statement, try: "I hear you saying you're fine. I'm also noticing you seem quieter than usual. I'm here if anything changes."

When they minimize problems: Rather than insisting the problem is bigger than they're acknowledging, try: "Even if it's not a big deal to you, I care about how you're doing."

When they take excessive responsibility: Instead of arguing about whose fault something is, try: "I appreciate that you want to fix this. Let's figure it out together."

When they deflect with humor or subject changes: Rather than forcing them back to the topic, try: "I notice we moved away from talking about that. We don't have to discuss it now, but I want you to know I care about how you're feeling."

This approach acknowledges both levels of communication - the words they feel safe saying and the emotional experience they can't directly express.

Modified Conversation Techniques

The GENTLE approach:

G - Give space for silence: Don't rush to fill quiet moments. Sometimes your partner needs time to access their emotional experience.

E - Express without expecting: Share your own feelings and observations without requiring reciprocation or response.

N - Notice without analyzing: Observe changes in mood or energy without demanding explanations.

T - Time your conversations: Choose moments when your partner seems most regulated and available rather than pushing for connection during stressed periods.

L - Listen to what's not said: Pay attention to emotional undertones, body language, and behavioral patterns.

E - Encourage without pursuing: Let your partner know you're available for deeper connection without pressuring them to open up before they're ready.

This modified approach honors your partner's emotional protection system while still creating opportunities for authentic connection.

Navigating Emotional Shutdown

When your partner goes into emotional shutdown mode, traditional relationship advice about "fighting for your relationship" or "not letting them push you away" can actually make things worse.

Shutdown is often a trauma response that requires a completely different approach.

What emotional shutdown looks like:

- Sudden unavailability or distance
- Minimal responses to questions or conversation attempts
- Physical presence but emotional absence
- Appearing confused or blank when asked about feelings
- Seeming to "disappear" even while in the same room

How to respond to shutdown:

- Don't take it personally (easier said than done, but crucial)
- Maintain your normal routines and energy
- Offer gentle, non-demanding support
- Give them space without withdrawing your availability
- Focus on your own emotional regulation during these periods

What not to do during shutdown:

- Demand explanations or emotional availability
- Pursue or chase them emotionally
- Interpret their withdrawal as rejection
- Make threats or ultimatums about their emotional unavailability
- Try to force them back to connection before they're ready

Think of shutdown as your partner's nervous system protecting them from perceived emotional threat. Your job isn't to override their protection system but to demonstrate that the threat isn't real.

Building Connection Through Shared Activities

Since direct emotional conversation can feel threatening, building intimacy through shared experiences often works better for people with quiet BPD. Connection can develop through activities that don't require vulnerability but create positive shared memories.

Low-pressure connection opportunities:

- Cooking or preparing meals together

- Taking walks or engaging in gentle physical activity

- Working on projects or creative activities side by side

- Watching movies or shows that might naturally open emotional conversations

- Engaging in routine activities together (grocery shopping, household tasks)

The key is creating opportunities for natural interaction without the pressure of forced emotional intimacy. Connection often develops more easily through parallel activities than through direct emotional conversation.

A Real-World Communication Journey

Consider a nurse whose partner worked in accounting. The accountant appeared emotionally stable and handled stress well, but the nurse noticed they rarely shared feelings or reactions to significant events. When asked directly about emotions, the accountant would seem genuinely confused or would minimize their experience.

Initially, the nurse tried standard communication advice: asking more questions, expressing frustration about lack of emotional sharing, and encouraging their partner to be more open. These approaches consistently led to increased withdrawal and distance.

The turning point came when the nurse shifted their approach entirely. Instead of pursuing emotional conversation, they began sharing their own feelings without expecting reciprocation. Instead of asking "How do you feel about this?" they started saying "I'm feeling worried about this situation" or "I'm excited about our plans."

They also began responding to their partner's actions rather than waiting for verbal communication. When the accountant seemed stressed, the nurse would handle extra household tasks or prepare favorite meals without discussing the stress directly. When the accountant appeared withdrawn, the nurse would maintain their availability without pursuing emotional connection.

Over time, this approach created enough safety for the accountant to begin sharing small emotional observations. They started mentioning when work felt overwhelming or when they appreciated something the nurse had done. Eventually, they were able to discuss their fear that emotional expression would burden others or lead to rejection.

The breakthrough wasn't dramatic - it was gradual building of trust through consistent, non-demanding emotional availability. The accountant learned that sharing feelings didn't automatically lead to criticism or increased expectations. The nurse learned that patience and indirect connection often work better than direct emotional pursuit.

Creating Your Communication Toolkit

Daily practices for better connection:

Morning check-ins: Share your own energy and intentions for the day without asking your partner to do the same. "I'm feeling pretty good today and looking forward to dinner together tonight."

Appreciation without reciprocity: Express gratitude for things your partner does without expecting them to return the sentiment. "I really appreciate how you handled that situation today."

Gentle observations: Notice positive things about your partner without making it about their emotional state. "You seem to be enjoying that book" rather than "You seem happier today."

Emotional modeling: Share appropriate feelings about neutral topics. "I'm frustrated with this traffic" or "I'm excited about the weekend."

End-of-day presence: Be available for connection without demanding it. Sit together, engage in parallel activities, or simply be present without conversation requirements.

Working With Emotional Flooding

Sometimes your partner might experience the opposite of shutdown - emotional flooding where feelings become overwhelming and dysregulated. This is still part of quiet BPD, just the internal experience breaking through their usual control.

Signs of emotional flooding:

- Seeming overwhelmed by normal situations

- Rapid speech or scattered thoughts

- Crying that seems disproportionate to the trigger

- Expressing fears or concerns that seem extreme

- Difficulty processing information or making decisions

How to respond to flooding:

- Stay calm and grounded yourself

- Use gentle, soothing voice tones

- Avoid trying to logic them out of their emotional experience

- Offer physical comfort if they're receptive

- Help them return to baseline through grounding techniques

Grounding techniques you can suggest:

- Deep breathing together

- Naming five things they can see, four they can hear, three they can touch

- Cold water on hands or face

- Going outside or changing physical location

- Gentle movement or stretching

The goal is helping your partner's nervous system return to regulation rather than trying to solve whatever triggered the flooding.

Setting Healthy Communication Boundaries

While you want to support your partner's emotional growth, you also need to protect your own emotional well-being. This means setting boundaries around communication that honor both people's needs.

Healthy boundaries might include:

"I want to support you, and I also need to know that my emotional needs matter in this relationship."

"I'm happy to give you space when you're struggling, and I also need you to let me know roughly how long you might need so I can plan accordingly."

"I understand that sharing feelings is difficult for you. I also need some emotional connection in our relationship, even if it starts small."

"I won't pressure you to talk when you're not ready, and I also won't pretend that everything is fine when I can sense you're struggling."

These boundaries protect your emotional well-being while still creating space for your partner's growth and healing.

When Communication Isn't Enough

Sometimes individual therapy becomes necessary for your partner to develop the emotional tools needed for authentic relationship communication. You can't therapy your partner into emotional availability, and attempting to do so often backfires.

Signs that professional help might be needed:

- Communication patterns aren't improving despite consistent effort from both people

- Your partner seems genuinely unable to access or express emotions

- Emotional shutdown periods are becoming longer or more frequent

- You're becoming emotionally depleted from one-sided communication efforts

- Your partner expresses interest in changing communication patterns but seems unable to make progress

Supporting your partner in seeking professional help isn't giving up on your relationship - it's recognizing that some healing requires specialized support that partners can't provide for each other.

The Evolution of Authentic Connection

Communication in quiet BPD relationships doesn't become "normal" overnight, but it can become authentic and satisfying with time and patience. Your partner can learn that emotional expression doesn't automatically lead to rejection. You can learn to distinguish between supporting growth and managing someone else's emotions.

The goal isn't perfect communication but real connection. This might look different from other relationships - perhaps more indirect, more gradual, more carefully paced. But it can be genuine, intimate, and deeply satisfying when both people understand and respect each other's emotional needs and limitations.

True intimacy becomes possible when your partner no longer has to choose between being authentic and feeling safe. Creating that safety is a joint project that requires patience, understanding, and commitment from both people.

With this foundation established, you're ready to explore the specific challenge of maintaining your emotional center while supporting someone who struggles to recognize and express their own needs - without losing yourself in the process.

Chapter 5: Mind Reading Isn't Love

You've become an expert at interpreting subtle signs, reading between lines, and anticipating needs that are never directly expressed. You pride yourself on knowing when your partner needs space, when they're struggling, and what will help them feel better - often before they know it themselves. This feels like love, like the ultimate expression of care and attuniveness.

But here's the uncomfortable truth: you're exhausting yourself trying to meet needs that haven't been communicated while your partner remains disconnected from their own emotional experience. You're both trapped in a cycle where unspoken expectations replace authentic communication, and mind reading substitutes for genuine emotional intimacy.

This dynamic isn't sustainable, and it isn't actually love - it's a form of codependency that keeps both people stuck. Your partner doesn't learn to identify and express their needs, and you lose touch with your own emotional center while constantly focusing on managing someone else's internal experience.

The Unspoken Expectations Trap

People with quiet BPD often develop what we might call "telepathic expectations" - they expect others to sense their needs without having to risk the vulnerability of expressing them directly. This isn't manipulation in the traditional sense; it's a survival strategy developed by someone who learned that direct emotional expression leads to rejection or criticism.

How unspoken expectations develop:

Your partner experiences intense emotions but has learned these feelings are dangerous to express. Instead of risking direct communication, they hope you'll notice their distress and respond appropriately. When you do notice and respond, it reinforces the pattern - they get their needs met without having to be vulnerable.

Over time, this creates a relationship dynamic where your partner expects you to be constantly attuned to their internal experience while they remain disconnected from it themselves. You become responsible for emotional awareness that rightfully belongs to them.

Common unspoken expectations:

- You should know when they need comfort without them asking

- You should sense when they need space without them saying so

- You should anticipate what will trigger their withdrawal and prevent it

- You should manage your own emotions to avoid overwhelming them

- You should provide reassurance for fears they won't directly express

The problem isn't that you care about your partner's emotional experience - healthy relationships require attunement and sensitivity. The problem is when this attunement becomes your primary job while your partner remains passive in their own emotional life.

The Emotional Labor Imbalance

In healthy relationships, emotional labor gets shared: both people work to understand their own emotions, communicate their needs, and respond supportively to their partner. In quiet BPD relationships, this labor often becomes severely imbalanced.

What you end up carrying:

- Monitoring and managing the emotional atmosphere for both people

- Translating your partner's indirect communications into actual needs
- Regulating your own emotions while managing theirs
- Taking responsibility for preventing triggers you can't identify
- Providing support while receiving little emotional reciprocity

What your partner avoids:

- Learning to identify and name their emotions
- Taking responsibility for communicating their needs
- Developing emotional regulation skills
- Offering emotional support when you need it
- Participating actively in relationship maintenance

This imbalance often develops gradually and feels natural because you're good at reading emotional cues and your partner seems to need the support. But over time, it creates resentment, exhaustion, and a relationship where only one person is emotionally present.

Breaking the Mind Reading Cycle

The first step in changing this dynamic is recognizing that mind reading isn't actually helpful for your partner's growth or your relationship's health. When you consistently anticipate and meet unspoken needs, you prevent your partner from developing emotional awareness and communication skills.

Practical steps to break the cycle:

Stop anticipating needs that haven't been expressed: When you notice your partner seems stressed, resist the urge to immediately fix or address the stress. Instead, stay available without taking action.

Ask for direct communication: "I'm noticing you seem upset. If you'd like support, let me know what would help." This puts the responsibility for identifying and communicating needs back where it belongs.

Don't interpret silence as consent: If your partner doesn't express preferences about plans, decisions, or activities, don't assume they're fine with whatever you choose. Ask directly and wait for actual answers.

Validate without rescuing: You can acknowledge that your partner seems to be struggling without immediately jumping in to fix or soothe. "I can see you're having a hard time" doesn't require action beyond acknowledgment.

Express your own needs clearly: Model the direct communication you want to receive. Share your emotions, state your preferences, and ask for specific support when you need it.

This approach might initially create more tension because your partner will need to develop skills they've been avoiding. But it's the only way to create genuine emotional reciprocity in your relationship.

The Difference Between Support and Enabling

Supporting someone with quiet BPD means helping them develop emotional awareness and communication skills. Enabling means doing their emotional work for them, which prevents growth and creates dependency.

Support looks like:

- Encouraging them to identify what they're feeling

- Asking what kind of help they need rather than assuming

- Validating their emotions while holding them responsible for expressing needs

- Being emotionally available without being emotionally responsible

- Setting boundaries around emotional labor that protect your own well-being

Enabling looks like:

- Consistently anticipating and meeting unspoken needs

- Managing their emotions for them

- Taking responsibility for preventing their emotional distress

- Accepting indirect communication instead of encouraging direct expression

- Sacrificing your own emotional needs to accommodate their avoidance

The difference isn't always obvious, especially when your partner seems to need significant support. The key question is: "Is what I'm doing helping them develop emotional skills, or is it preventing them from learning those skills?"

Practical Communication Strategies

The direct request approach: Instead of anticipating needs, wait for direct requests. When your partner seems to need something, say: "If you'd like my support with something, let me know specifically what would help."

The emotional check-in method: Create regular opportunities for emotional sharing that don't depend on crisis or subtle cues. "I'd like to hear how you're doing emotionally" followed by genuine listening without immediate problem-solving.

The needs clarification technique: When your partner communicates indirectly, ask for clarification rather than interpreting. "When you say you're fine, are you letting me know you don't need support right now, or are you saying something else?"

The emotional modeling practice: Demonstrate direct communication by sharing your own needs clearly. "I'm feeling overwhelmed today and would appreciate help with dinner" or "I need some quiet time this evening to recharge."

The response timing strategy: When your partner expresses needs indirectly, don't respond immediately. Give them time to express themselves more directly by saying, "Let me think about what you've shared and get back to you."

These strategies gradually shift the responsibility for emotional awareness and communication back to your partner while maintaining your supportive availability.

Dealing with Resistance to Direct Communication

Your partner might resist taking more responsibility for their emotional communication, especially if they've been relying on your mind reading abilities for a long time. This resistance often comes from fear rather than laziness or manipulation.

Common forms of resistance:

- Insisting they shouldn't have to ask for basic support
- Becoming more withdrawn when you stop anticipating needs
- Expressing frustration that you're not as attentive as before
- Claiming they don't know what they need or feel
- Reverting to more indirect communication during stress

How to respond to resistance:

- Stay compassionate while maintaining boundaries
- Explain that you're asking for direct communication because you care about the relationship
- Acknowledge that learning new communication skills is difficult

- Remain consistent with your new approach even when it feels uncomfortable

- Focus on long-term relationship health rather than short-term harmony

The resistance usually decreases once your partner realizes that direct communication actually leads to better support and deeper connection than mind reading ever could.

A Real-World Transformation Story

Consider a physical therapist whose partner worked in graphic design. The designer rarely expressed needs directly but had developed subtle ways of communicating distress: working late when feeling overwhelmed, cleaning obsessively when anxious, or becoming unusually quiet when needing reassurance.

The physical therapist had become expert at reading these signals and responding appropriately. When the designer worked late, they'd prepare dinner and handle household tasks. When the designer cleaned obsessively, they'd suggest relaxing activities. When the designer became quiet, they'd provide extra affection and reassurance.

This system seemed to work until the physical therapist realized they were constantly managing emotional dynamics for both people while receiving little emotional support in return. They felt like an emotional detective, always analyzing clues and trying to solve mysteries they hadn't been asked to solve.

The change began when the physical therapist stopped responding automatically to indirect communications. Instead of immediately adjusting their behavior when the designer seemed distressed, they started asking direct questions: "I notice you're working late again. Are you feeling overwhelmed with the project, or is something else going on?"

Initially, the designer resisted this approach, insisting they were "fine" and didn't need to discuss their feelings. The physical therapist maintained their caring availability while refusing to interpret or act on unspoken cues.

Over several months, the designer gradually began expressing needs more directly. They started saying things like "I'm feeling anxious about this deadline and could use some encouragement" instead of just working late and hoping for automatic support.

The breakthrough moment came when the designer realized that direct communication actually led to better support than indirect signals ever had. When they asked specifically for what they needed, they got exactly that type of help rather than the physical therapist's best guess about what might help.

This shift transformed their relationship dynamic. The physical therapist felt less emotionally exhausted and more genuinely helpful. The designer developed better emotional awareness and felt more confident about getting their needs met.

Setting Boundaries Around Emotional Labor

Creating balance in emotional labor requires setting clear boundaries about what you will and won't take responsibility for in the relationship.

Boundaries around emotional responsibility:

- "I care about how you're feeling, and I need you to share that information directly rather than expecting me to guess."

- "I'm happy to provide support when you ask for it specifically. I'm not going to try to anticipate needs that haven't been expressed."

- "I can't be responsible for managing your emotions, and I don't expect you to manage mine."

- "When you're struggling, I want to help in ways that actually work rather than guessing what might help."

Boundaries around communication:

- "I need direct answers to direct questions, even if the answer is 'I don't know' or 'I need time to think.'"

- "When you say you're fine, I'm going to believe you unless you tell me otherwise."

- "I can't read your mind, and I don't want you to try to read mine. Let's use words instead."

These boundaries protect your emotional energy while encouraging your partner to develop healthier communication patterns.

Teaching Through Modeling

One of the most effective ways to encourage direct communication is through consistent modeling of healthy emotional expression.

How to model emotional directness:

Share your feelings clearly: "I'm feeling frustrated about this situation" rather than expecting your partner to sense your mood.

Ask for specific support: "I could use a hug right now" or "I need someone to listen while I talk through this problem."

Express appreciation directly: "I really appreciated when you handled the dishes yesterday. It helped me relax after a stressful day."

Communicate boundaries kindly: "I need some quiet time this evening" rather than hoping your partner will sense your need for space.

Express preferences clearly: "I'd prefer to stay home tonight" instead of saying "whatever you want" when you actually have a preference.

When your partner sees that direct communication leads to better understanding and connection, they're more likely to try it themselves.

The Long-Term Benefits of Breaking the Cycle

Ending the unspoken expectations cycle creates benefits for both people and the relationship as a whole.

Benefits for your partner:

- Develops emotional awareness and communication skills
- Learns to identify and express needs appropriately
- Builds confidence in their ability to maintain relationships through authentic communication
- Experiences the satisfaction of genuine emotional reciprocity
- Reduces the shame that comes from feeling like a burden

Benefits for you:

- Reduces emotional exhaustion from constant mind reading
- Allows you to provide support that actually helps rather than guessing
- Frees up emotional energy for your own needs and growth
- Creates space for genuine emotional intimacy
- Builds a relationship based on authentic communication rather than assumptions

Benefits for the relationship:

- Creates genuine emotional reciprocity instead of one-sided caretaking
- Builds trust through direct, honest communication
- Reduces misunderstandings and unmet expectations
- Allows both people to be authentic rather than performing roles
- Creates a foundation for long-term growth and intimacy

Navigating the Transition Period

Changing established communication patterns takes time and often feels uncomfortable initially. Both people need to adjust to new ways of relating that might feel foreign or challenging.

What to expect during the transition:

- Initial resistance from your partner who's used to indirect communication

- Temporary increase in relationship tension as old patterns get disrupted

- Moments when you're tempted to return to mind reading because it feels easier

- Gradual improvement in communication clarity and emotional connection

- Growing confidence in both people's ability to express needs directly

How to stay committed during difficult moments:

- Remember that discomfort often precedes growth

- Focus on long-term relationship health rather than short-term ease

- Celebrate small improvements in direct communication

- Seek support from friends, family, or professionals when needed

- Trust that authentic communication leads to deeper intimacy than mind reading ever could

Creating Your Communication Agreement

Consider developing explicit agreements about communication expectations that both people can commit to.

Sample communication agreements:

"We both commit to expressing our needs directly rather than expecting mind reading."

"When one of us is struggling, we'll ask for specific support rather than hoping the other person will guess what helps."

"We'll both work on developing emotional awareness and sharing that information appropriately."

"If we need space or time to process, we'll communicate that directly rather than withdrawing without explanation."

"We'll both take responsibility for our own emotional regulation while remaining available to support each other when asked."

Having explicit agreements helps both people stay committed to healthier communication patterns, especially during challenging moments.

Mind reading isn't love - it's a barrier to authentic intimacy. When you stop trying to anticipate every need and start asking for direct communication, you create space for genuine emotional connection to develop. Your partner learns to participate actively in their own emotional life, and you learn to provide support that actually helps rather than guessing what might work.

This groundwork prepares us for exploring what happens when your partner's emotional withdrawal triggers crisis responses in you, and how to support someone through internal storms without losing yourself in the process.

Chapter 6: Crisis Intervention When the Crisis Is Invisible

Crisis in quiet BPD relationships doesn't announce itself with dramatic outbursts or visible self-destructive behavior. Instead, it whispers through subtle changes in routine, creeps in through emotional numbness, and hides behind increased perfectionism or sudden withdrawal. You might sense that something is terribly wrong while your partner insists they're fine, leaving you to navigate the challenging territory of supporting someone through a crisis they won't acknowledge or can't recognize.

Traditional crisis intervention assumes visible distress signals and direct requests for help. With quiet BPD, you're often dealing with someone who's in genuine emotional danger while maintaining their usual outward composure. This creates unique challenges: How do you help someone who won't admit they need help? How do you intervene in a crisis that looks like calmness? How do you balance respect for their autonomy with genuine concern for their safety?

The key lies in understanding that internal crises can be just as serious as external ones, while learning to recognize subtle danger signs that traditional crisis training might miss entirely.

Recognizing Invisible Crisis Signals

When someone internalizes their emotional distress, crisis doesn't look like what most people expect. There's no dramatic breakdown, no obvious call for help, no visible signs of self-destruction. Instead, crisis manifests through subtle changes that might be easily dismissed as stress, tiredness, or normal mood fluctuation.

Hidden crisis indicators:

Increased emotional numbing: Your partner seems unusually disconnected from their emotions, responding to both positive and negative events with the same flat affect.

Perfectionism escalation: Normal attention to detail becomes rigid control over environment, appearance, or performance that seems disproportionate to the situation.

Social withdrawal disguised as independence: Your partner cancels social plans, avoids family contact, or declines activities they usually enjoy, framing it as being busy or needing alone time.

Routine disruption without explanation: Changes in sleep, eating, exercise, or daily habits that seem to have no external cause.

Internal self-harm indicators: Increased self-critical comments, mentions of feeling "empty" or "numb," or expressions of guilt and worthlessness that seem excessive.

Dissociation signs: Seeming confused about time, having difficulty concentrating, or appearing "spacey" or disconnected from their immediate environment.

Future-focused anxiety: Sudden preoccupation with worst-case scenarios, making detailed preparations for disasters that seem unlikely, or expressing certainty that bad things will happen.

The challenge is that these signs often get rationalized away by both the person experiencing them and their partner. "They're just stressed" or "They've always been detail-oriented" can mask genuine emotional crisis.

Understanding Internal Self-Harm

One of the most concerning aspects of quiet BPD crisis is that self-destructive behaviors remain entirely internal and invisible to others. While external self-harm creates obvious cause for concern, internal self-harm can be equally damaging while remaining completely hidden.

Forms of internal self-harm during crisis:

Emotional self-punishment: Relentless internal criticism, self-blame for things outside their control, or mental rehearsal of past mistakes and failures.

Deliberate emotional deprivation: Denying themselves comfort, connection, or activities that bring joy as a form of self-punishment.

Overwhelming responsibility-taking: Assuming blame for other people's emotions, problems, or life circumstances as a way of confirming their internal belief that they're fundamentally flawed.

Isolation as punishment: Withdrawing from supportive relationships because they believe they don't deserve care or will burden others with their presence.

Identity erasure: Losing touch with their own preferences, needs, and desires while focusing exclusively on meeting others' expectations.

Perfectionism as self-attack: Setting impossible standards and then using inevitable failures as evidence of their worthlessness.

These internal behaviors can create genuine risk of suicide or self-harm without any external warning signs that traditional crisis training would recognize.

When Professional Help Becomes Necessary

Sometimes crisis intervention requires professional support that partners can't provide alone. Recognizing when this level of help is needed can be life-saving.

Clear indicators for professional intervention:

Direct or indirect references to suicide: Any mention of wanting to die, feeling like others would be better off without them, or references to ending their life.

Severe dissociation: Significant confusion about time, place, or identity that interferes with daily functioning.

Complete emotional shutdown: Total inability to access or express emotions for extended periods, especially if accompanied by other concerning behaviors.

Dangerous self-neglect: Stopping eating, sleeping, personal hygiene, or medical care in ways that threaten physical health.

Inability to function: Can't work, maintain relationships, or handle basic life responsibilities for extended periods.

Expressing hopelessness: Statements that nothing will ever get better, that they're permanently broken, or that there's no point in trying.

Increased risk-taking: Driving recklessly, using substances, or engaging in behaviors that seem designed to cause harm without appearing intentionally self-destructive.

When these signs appear, professional crisis intervention becomes necessary regardless of your partner's willingness to acknowledge the severity of their situation.

Creating Safety Plans for Invisible Crisis

Traditional safety planning assumes the person in crisis can identify their triggers and warning signs. With quiet BPD, safety planning needs to account for someone who might not recognize their own crisis states or might be unable to ask for help directly.

Modified safety planning approach:

External observation indicators: Since your partner might not recognize their own warning signs, include behavioral changes that you or others might notice - withdrawal patterns, routine changes, or emotional numbing.

Indirect communication strategies: Plan for how your partner can signal distress without having to say "I'm in crisis" directly. This might include code words, text messages, or specific behaviors that indicate they need support.

Support person protocols: Establish clear agreements about when you or others should step in, even if your partner hasn't directly asked for help.

Professional contact information: Keep readily available contact information for crisis hotlines, emergency services, and mental health professionals who understand quiet BPD presentations.

Environmental safety measures: Remove or secure potentially harmful items during crisis periods, even if your partner hasn't expressed direct self-harm intentions.

Grounding and regulation tools: Identify specific techniques that help your partner return to emotional baseline during crisis, such as sensory grounding, breathing exercises, or physical comfort measures.

Your Role During Invisible Crisis

Supporting someone through invisible crisis requires delicate balance between respecting their autonomy and ensuring their safety. You can't force someone to acknowledge crisis, but you can create conditions that support their survival and recovery.

Effective crisis support strategies:

Stay calm and grounded yourself: Your emotional regulation helps create stability when your partner's internal world feels chaotic.

Increase your presence without being intrusive: Be more available and attentive without demanding explanations or emotional access.

Handle practical responsibilities: Take care of daily tasks that might feel overwhelming during crisis - meals, bills, household management.

Provide gentle physical comfort: Offer hugs, hand-holding, or simply sitting near them if they're receptive to physical connection.

Limit decision-making demands: Reduce the number of choices your partner needs to make when their emotional resources are depleted.

Monitor without interrogating: Keep track of concerning behaviors without constantly asking how they're feeling or what they need.

Maintain routine and normalcy: Keep regular schedules and activities going to provide stability and structure.

The goal is creating a supportive environment that promotes healing without forcing your partner to be more emotionally available than they can safely manage during crisis.

Communication During Crisis Periods

Normal communication strategies often need modification during quiet BPD crisis periods. Your partner might be even less able to express emotions directly, requiring more patience and creativity in maintaining connection.

Crisis communication approaches:

Use simple, clear language: Avoid complex conversations or decisions that might feel overwhelming when emotional resources are limited.

Offer specific support options: Instead of "What do you need?" try "Would it help if I made dinner?" or "Would you like me to handle the grocery shopping this week?"

Validate without requiring response: "I can see you're going through something difficult. You don't need to talk about it, but I want you to know I'm here."

Check in without demanding answers: "I'm thinking about you" or "I care about how you're doing" without expecting detailed responses.

Respect increased need for space: Allow for more alone time while maintaining your availability for connection when they're ready.

Avoid pushing for emotional processing: Crisis periods aren't the time for deep emotional conversations or relationship processing.

Remember that during crisis, your partner's ability to communicate might be even more limited than usual. Patience and reduced expectations around emotional availability become especially important.

Supporting Recovery Without Enabling

The period following invisible crisis requires careful balance between supporting healing and encouraging healthy coping skill development. You want to help your partner recover while avoiding patterns that prevent them from developing their own emotional resilience.

Recovery support that promotes growth:

Encourage professional help without demanding it: "I think talking to someone might be helpful" while respecting their autonomy about seeking treatment.

Support healthy coping strategies: Encourage activities, relationships, and habits that promote emotional regulation and well-being.

Gradually increase expectations: Slowly return to normal relationship expectations as your partner's emotional capacity recovers.

Process the crisis experience when they're ready: When appropriate, discuss what happened and what might help prevent or manage future crisis periods.

Celebrate small improvements: Acknowledge progress in emotional awareness, communication, or coping without making it about your own relief.

Avoiding recovery enabling:

Don't take permanent responsibility for crisis prevention: You can't and shouldn't try to manage your partner's emotional life to prevent future crisis.

Avoid becoming their emotional safety net: Support their development of multiple coping strategies rather than becoming their primary regulation tool.

Don't ignore your own needs during recovery: Maintain your own emotional health and seek support for the stress of supporting someone through crisis.

Resist the urge to control their healing process: Allow your partner to recover at their own pace using methods that work for them.

A Real-World Crisis Navigation Story

Consider a teacher whose partner worked as a software developer. The developer had always been emotionally reserved but seemed to be managing life well - maintaining good work performance, keeping up with responsibilities, and appearing generally stable.

Over several weeks, the teacher noticed subtle changes that seemed minor individually but created a concerning pattern when viewed together. The developer stopped mentioning work colleagues, declined social invitations without explanation, and began spending excessive time organizing areas of their home that were already clean.

When asked directly, the developer insisted everything was fine and seemed genuinely confused by the teacher's concerns. They maintained their normal routines and continued handling responsibilities effectively, making the teacher wonder if they were overreacting to normal stress patterns.

The situation escalated when the teacher found evidence of the developer researching methods of self-harm online, while still maintaining their usual calm exterior and insisting they felt fine. This discrepancy between internal crisis and external presentation helped the teacher recognize they were dealing with invisible crisis that required intervention.

Instead of confronting the developer directly about the research (which might have increased shame and secrecy), the teacher began implementing subtle crisis support measures. They increased their presence without being intrusive, handled extra household responsibilities, and created opportunities for low-pressure connection.

The teacher also quietly removed potentially harmful items from their home and researched crisis resources in case professional intervention became necessary. They maintained normal routines while being more attentive to changes in the developer's behavior and mood.

The breakthrough came when the teacher expressed concern in a non-threatening way: "I've noticed you seem to be going through something difficult lately. I don't need to know details, but I want you to know I'm here and I care about your well-being."

This opened space for the developer to eventually share that they'd been experiencing intense thoughts of self-harm and feelings of worthlessness that felt overwhelming and shameful. They'd been trying to handle these feelings alone because admitting to crisis felt like failure.

With professional support, the developer learned to recognize early warning signs of crisis and develop healthier coping strategies. The teacher learned to trust their instincts about concerning changes while respecting their partner's autonomy and privacy.

Building Your Crisis Response Skills

Developing crisis awareness:

Trust your instincts: If something feels off about your partner's emotional state, take those concerns seriously even if there's no obvious evidence of crisis.

Look for patterns rather than isolated incidents: Multiple small changes might indicate crisis more clearly than any single dramatic event.

Learn your partner's specific crisis signals: Each person with quiet BPD might have unique ways that crisis manifests behaviorally.

Stay educated about quiet BPD crisis presentations: Understanding how internal crisis differs from external crisis helps you recognize concerning changes.

Preparing for crisis situations:

Know your resources: Have contact information for crisis hotlines, emergency services, and mental health professionals readily available.

Understand legal and ethical considerations: Know when you might need to involve others in crisis intervention, even without your partner's consent.

Develop your own support system: Supporting someone through crisis is stressful and requires your own sources of support and guidance.

Practice emotional regulation: Your ability to stay calm during crisis directly impacts your effectiveness in providing support.

Creating Long-Term Crisis Prevention

While you can't prevent all crisis situations, understanding your partner's patterns and triggers can help create conditions that reduce crisis frequency and intensity.

Prevention strategies:

Reduce overall stress levels: Help create lifestyle patterns that don't overwhelm your partner's emotional capacity.

Encourage consistent self-care: Support habits that promote emotional regulation like adequate sleep, exercise, and nutrition.

Build support networks: Encourage connections with friends, family, or professionals that provide emotional resources beyond just your relationship.

Develop early intervention skills: Learn to recognize and respond to early warning signs before they develop into full crisis.

Address underlying triggers: Work together (potentially with professional help) to understand and address root causes of crisis patterns.

The goal isn't eliminating all emotional difficulties but creating resilience and resources that help your partner navigate challenges without reaching crisis levels.

Crisis intervention in quiet BPD relationships requires patience, intuition, and willingness to act on concerns that might not be obviously justified. Trusting your instincts about your partner's well-being, while respecting their autonomy and privacy, creates the foundation for effective crisis support that can literally save lives.

These discoveries lead us naturally to exploring the professional therapeutic resources that can provide specialized support for quiet BPD, and how to navigate the mental health system when symptoms remain largely invisible to outside observers.

Chapter 7: Finding the Right Help for The Overcontrolled Mind

The mental health system isn't designed for people who look fine on the surface. Most therapists are trained to recognize obvious distress signals - dramatic emotions, clear behavioral problems, or direct requests for help. When your partner appears calm, functional, and emotionally stable while struggling with internal chaos, finding appropriate professional support becomes a unique challenge.

Traditional therapy approaches often assume that people can identify and express their emotions, recognize their patterns, and actively participate in treatment discussions. For someone with quiet BPD, these assumptions don't hold true. Your partner might sit through sessions insisting they're fine while experiencing internal emotional turmoil. They might complete therapy homework perfectly while missing the point entirely. They might appear to be an ideal client while gaining no actual benefit from treatment.

Understanding what therapeutic approaches actually work for overcontrolled personalities - and how to find professionals who understand these presentations - can make the difference between years of ineffective treatment and genuine healing and growth.

Why Standard Approaches Often Miss the Mark

Most therapy models are designed for people who are emotionally expressive, can identify their feelings, and are motivated to explore their internal experience. Quiet BPD presents the opposite challenge: someone who has learned to suppress emotions so effectively that even they don't know what they're feeling.

Where traditional therapy falls short:

Emotion-focused approaches assume emotional access: Many therapy models require people to identify and express feelings, but someone with quiet BPD might genuinely not know what they're experiencing emotionally.

Insight-oriented therapy requires self-awareness: Traditional talk therapy assumes people can recognize their patterns and motivations, but overcontrol often creates blind spots about internal experience.

Standard CBT targets obvious thought patterns: While cognitive behavioral therapy can be helpful, it often focuses on thoughts and behaviors that are visible and accessible, missing the internal emotional dysregulation that drives quiet BPD.

Group therapy assumes comfort with emotional expression: Many therapeutic programs involve sharing feelings with others, which can feel impossible for someone who's spent years hiding their emotional experience.

Crisis-oriented treatment misses invisible distress: Mental health systems often respond to obvious crises while missing people who are suffering intensely without visible symptoms.

Your partner might complete months or years of therapy that feels helpful in the moment but doesn't address the core emotional dysregulation that's creating relationship and life difficulties.

Understanding Radically Open DBT

Dr. Thomas Lynch developed Radically Open Dialectical Behavior Therapy (RO-DBT) specifically for people with overcontrolled personalities - including those with quiet BPD presentations. Unlike standard DBT, which focuses on helping people gain more control over their emotions, RO-DBT helps people learn to be more emotionally open and flexible.

Key differences from standard DBT:

Targets overcontrol rather than undercontrol: Instead of teaching emotional regulation to people who are emotionally explosive, RO-

DBT helps people who have too much emotional control learn appropriate emotional expression.

Focuses on social connection: The therapy emphasizes learning to connect with others through appropriate emotional expression rather than maintaining emotional walls.

Addresses perfectionism and rigidity: RO-DBT specifically targets the perfectionism and inflexibility that often characterize quiet BPD presentations.

Emphasizes authentic self-expression: The approach helps people learn that emotional vulnerability can actually strengthen relationships rather than destroy them.

Includes skills for increasing emotional expression: Rather than learning to contain emotions, clients learn when and how to express emotions appropriately.

Core RO-DBT principles relevant to quiet BPD:

Emotional expression as social signaling: Learning that sharing emotions appropriately helps others understand how to respond supportively.

Flexible responding to unexpected situations: Developing the ability to adapt when life doesn't go according to plan without emotional shutdown.

Social connection through vulnerability: Understanding that authentic emotional sharing creates deeper relationships than perfect performance.

For someone with quiet BPD, RO-DBT addresses the specific challenges of overcontrol while building skills that improve both individual well-being and relationship functioning.

Other Effective Therapeutic Approaches

While RO-DBT is specifically designed for overcontrolled presentations, other therapeutic approaches can also be effective when delivered by therapists who understand quiet BPD dynamics.

Schema Therapy for relationship patterns: This approach helps identify and change deep-rooted emotional patterns that developed in childhood. For quiet BPD, it often focuses on themes like emotional deprivation, defectiveness, and fear of abandonment.

Mentalization-Based Therapy (MBT) for emotional awareness: MBT helps people develop the ability to understand their own and others' emotional experiences. This can be particularly helpful for someone who has lost touch with their internal emotional world.

Emotion-Focused Therapy (EFT) for couples: When both partners are motivated, EFT can help address the attachment and emotional connection issues that characterize quiet BPD relationships.

Internal Family Systems (IFS) for the "split self" phenomenon: IFS helps people integrate different aspects of their personality, which can be particularly relevant for the "normal self" versus "wounded self" split common in quiet BPD.

The key is finding therapists who understand that the absence of obvious emotional expression doesn't mean the absence of emotional problems.

Finding Qualified Professionals

Locating mental health professionals who understand quiet BPD presentations requires more research than simply calling the first therapist with an available appointment.

Questions to ask potential therapists:

"Do you have experience working with people who have quiet or internalized BPD presentations?"

"How do you approach therapy with clients who have difficulty accessing or expressing emotions?"

"Are you familiar with overcontrolled personality patterns and RO-DBT approaches?"

"How do you handle clients who appear fine on the surface but struggle with internal emotional dysregulation?"

"What's your experience with people who have been in therapy before without significant improvement?"

Red flags in therapist responses:

- Dismissing the concept of quiet BPD or insisting all BPD presents dramatically

- Focusing only on standard DBT without understanding overcontrol

- Suggesting that if someone appears functional, they probably don't need intensive therapy

- Lack of familiarity with attachment-based or trauma-informed approaches

- Assumption that therapy progress should be obvious and linear

Positive indicators:

- Familiarity with quiet BPD, overcontrol, or RO-DBT concepts

- Understanding that emotional regulation problems can be invisible

- Experience with clients who have difficulty accessing emotions

- Comfort with slower therapy progress and subtle changes

- Integration of attachment and trauma approaches

Preparing Your Partner for Therapy

Someone with quiet BPD might resist therapy because they don't see themselves as having obvious problems, or they might have had previous therapy experiences that felt unhelpful or invalidating.

Common barriers to therapy engagement:

"I'm fine" resistance: Your partner might genuinely believe they don't need therapy because their problems are internal and invisible.

Previous therapy disappointments: If they've tried therapy before without benefit, they might be skeptical about trying again.

Fear of being "found out": Therapy requires emotional vulnerability that feels dangerous to someone who has learned to hide their feelings.

Perfectionism about being a "good client": They might worry about disappointing the therapist or doing therapy "wrong."

Control concerns: Therapy involves giving up some control and allowing another person to influence their internal experience.

Helpful approaches to therapy preparation:

Focus on relationship goals rather than individual pathology: Frame therapy as working on communication and connection rather than fixing something wrong with them.

Emphasize their choice and control: Make it clear that therapy is their decision and they can stop or change approaches at any time.

Discuss different therapy types: Explain that not all therapy is the same, and finding the right approach and therapist matters.

Address previous therapy experiences: If they've had unhelpful therapy before, acknowledge that experience while explaining how different approaches might be more effective.

Start small: Consider beginning with a few sessions to "try it out" rather than committing to long-term treatment initially.

Couple's Therapy Considerations

Couple's therapy can be incredibly helpful for quiet BPD relationships, but it requires therapists who understand the unique dynamics involved.

What effective couple's therapy addresses:

Communication patterns around emotional expression: Helping both partners learn to share and receive emotions more effectively.

The emotional labor imbalance: Addressing how to create more reciprocity in emotional support and relationship maintenance.

Attachment and connection issues: Working on the approach-avoidance patterns that characterize quiet BPD relationships.

Understanding rather than changing: Helping both partners understand quiet BPD dynamics rather than trying to force different behavior.

Couple's therapy approaches that work well:

Emotionally Focused Therapy (EFT): Focuses on attachment and emotional connection, which directly addresses quiet BPD relationship challenges.

Gottman Method: Emphasizes building friendship and managing conflict constructively, which can help address communication difficulties.

PREP (Prevention and Relationship Enhancement Program): Teaches specific communication skills that can benefit relationships where one partner struggles with emotional expression.

What to avoid in couple's therapy:

- Therapists who focus on blame or try to identify the "problem partner"

- Approaches that demand immediate emotional openness from your partner

- Therapy that doesn't understand trauma and attachment issues

- Treatment that pathologizes quiet BPD traits rather than working with them

Supporting Treatment Without Managing It

When your partner begins therapy, you might feel tempted to monitor their progress, encourage specific topics, or become involved in their treatment process. While support is important, managing their therapy often backfires.

Helpful support looks like:

Practical assistance: Helping with scheduling, transportation, or other logistics without discussing therapy content.

Emotional encouragement: Expressing belief in their ability to grow and change without pressuring for specific outcomes.

Patience with the process: Understanding that therapy progress might be slow and not always visible.

Maintaining your own growth: Working on your own patterns and needs rather than focusing exclusively on their treatment.

Celebrating small changes: Acknowledging improvements in communication or emotional expression without making it about your relief.

Unhelpful involvement includes:

- Asking detailed questions about therapy sessions

- Suggesting topics they should discuss with their therapist

- Monitoring their therapy homework or progress

- Feeling responsible for their engagement or success in treatment

- Using their therapy as leverage in relationship discussions

The goal is supporting their autonomy in healing rather than becoming another source of pressure or expectation.

A Real-World Treatment Journey

Consider an accountant whose partner was a social worker. The accountant had tried therapy twice before - once after a family member's death and once during a particularly stressful work period. Both experiences involved therapists who used standard talk therapy approaches, asking questions about feelings and encouraging emotional expression.

The accountant completed both therapy experiences successfully, attending all sessions and doing assigned homework. However, they reported feeling like they were "performing" therapy rather than actually benefiting from it. They could discuss their thoughts and behaviors intellectually but never felt like they were accessing their authentic emotional experience.

The social worker, who had experience with different therapy modalities through work, suggested they research therapists who specialized in attachment and trauma work. They found a therapist trained in both traditional DBT and RO-DBT who understood overcontrolled presentations.

The initial sessions focused on psychoeducation about overcontrol and quiet BPD rather than immediately pushing for emotional expression. The therapist explained how emotional suppression develops as a protective strategy and validated the accountant's experience of feeling disconnected from their emotions.

Rather than asking "How do you feel about that?" the therapist would say things like "That sounds like it might have been overwhelming" or "Many people in similar situations feel angry, even if they can't access that feeling directly."

The therapy included specific exercises for developing emotional awareness - body scans to notice physical sensations, mindfulness practices to observe internal experience without judgment, and gradual exposure to emotional expression in safe contexts.

Progress was slow and subtle. The accountant began noticing physical tension they hadn't been aware of before. They started recognizing that their "tiredness" often accompanied emotional situations. Eventually, they could identify basic emotions like frustration or sadness, even if expressing them still felt difficult.

The breakthrough came when the accountant realized they could share emotions with their therapist without negative consequences. This created a safe laboratory for practicing emotional expression before trying it in their relationship.

After eight months of therapy, the accountant was able to say things like "I'm feeling overwhelmed by work stress and could use some support" instead of just working late and hoping their partner would notice their distress.

When Individual Therapy Isn't Enough

Sometimes quiet BPD requires more intensive treatment than weekly individual therapy can provide.

Intensive outpatient programs (IOPs): Some programs specifically address overcontrolled personality patterns through group therapy, skills training, and individual sessions multiple times per week.

DBT skills groups: While traditional DBT groups might not be perfect for quiet BPD, some groups specifically address overcontrol or are facilitated by therapists who understand these presentations.

Therapeutic retreats or workshops: Intensive experiences focused on emotional awareness, attachment, or trauma can sometimes create breakthroughs that weekly therapy can't achieve.

Psychiatric evaluation: While medication isn't a cure for BPD, some people benefit from treatment for co-occurring conditions like depression or anxiety that might be complicating their emotional experience.

The key is finding intensive treatments that understand overcontrol rather than approaches designed for dramatic emotional presentations.

Insurance and Financial Considerations

Mental health treatment can be expensive, and insurance coverage for personality disorder treatment varies significantly.

Maximizing insurance coverage:

Focus on covered diagnoses: Insurance often covers treatment for depression or anxiety more readily than personality disorders.

Emphasize medical necessity: Document how symptoms interfere with daily functioning, work, or relationships.

Research your plan's mental health benefits: Understand what types of therapy, length of treatment, and provider types are covered.

Consider in-network versus out-of-network options: Sometimes paying more for a specialist who understands quiet BPD provides better value than covered treatment that doesn't help.

Alternative funding options:

- Therapist sliding scale fees
- Graduate training programs that offer reduced-cost therapy
- Employee assistance programs through work
- Community mental health centers
- Online therapy platforms that might be more affordable

Cost-benefit considerations: Effective therapy that addresses core issues might be more cost-effective than years of less expensive treatment that doesn't create meaningful change.

Measuring Progress in Quiet BPD Treatment

Progress in quiet BPD therapy often looks different from other types of mental health treatment. Changes might be subtle and develop slowly over months or years.

Signs of positive progress:

Increased emotional awareness: Ability to identify and name emotions, even if expressing them still feels difficult.

Improved relationship communication: More direct expression of needs and feelings, even in small ways.

Reduced perfectionism: Willingness to be "good enough" rather than perfect in some areas of life.

Better stress tolerance: Less likely to shut down completely during difficult situations.

Increased self-compassion: Treating themselves with more kindness and less internal criticism.

Greater emotional flexibility: Ability to adapt when plans change or unexpected situations arise.

What progress might NOT look like:

- Dramatic emotional breakthroughs or cathartic moments
- Sudden ability to express all emotions freely
- Elimination of all quiet BPD traits or characteristics
- Linear improvement without setbacks or difficult periods
- Immediate changes in long-standing relationship patterns

Understanding that progress is often gradual and subtle helps maintain realistic expectations while recognizing genuine improvement.

The right therapeutic support can transform quiet BPD from a relationship-destroying condition into an understandable pattern that both people can work with consciously and compassionately. Finding that support requires patience, research, and willingness to advocate for treatment approaches that address invisible emotional struggles.

Having established these principles, you're ready to explore your specific role in supporting your partner's healing journey while maintaining your own emotional well-being and avoiding the trap of becoming their unofficial therapist.

Chapter 8: Your Role in Their Healing (and what isn't your role)

Love makes us want to fix, heal, and solve the problems of people we care about. When your partner struggles with invisible emotional pain, the urge to become their primary source of support, understanding, and healing can feel not just natural but necessary. After all, you're the one who sees their hidden struggles, understands their patterns, and cares most about their well-being.

But here's what many partners don't realize: trying to be your partner's therapist, emotional manager, or healing facilitator often prevents the very growth and healing you're hoping to support. Well-intentioned attempts to "help them get better" can actually reinforce the patterns that keep them stuck, while exhausting your own emotional resources in the process.

Understanding the difference between supportive partnership and therapeutic overreach isn't just important for your partner's growth - it's essential for your own well-being and the health of your relationship as a whole.

The Therapeutic Boundary Line

The line between supportive partner and amateur therapist can be surprisingly easy to cross, especially when you understand your partner's struggles better than they do. But maintaining this boundary is crucial for both people's health and growth.

What partners can appropriately provide:

Emotional support and validation: Acknowledging your partner's struggles and expressing care for their well-being without trying to analyze or fix their emotions.

Practical assistance during difficult times: Taking on extra household responsibilities, managing logistics, or providing physical comfort when your partner is struggling.

Encouragement for professional help: Supporting their decision to seek therapy while respecting their autonomy about treatment choices.

Modeling healthy emotional expression: Demonstrating appropriate ways to share feelings and ask for support without lecturing or teaching.

Consistent presence and availability: Being emotionally available for connection without pursuing or demanding emotional access.

What crosses into therapeutic territory:

Analyzing their childhood or past trauma: Trying to help them understand how their history created current patterns.

Teaching emotional regulation skills: Attempting to guide them through mindfulness, breathing exercises, or other therapeutic techniques.

Interpreting their behavior or emotions: Telling them what they're "really" feeling or what their actions "actually" mean.

Setting therapeutic goals or monitoring progress: Deciding what they need to work on or tracking their emotional development.

Creating treatment plans or homework: Designing activities or exercises to help them grow emotionally.

The key difference is that partners provide emotional support within the relationship, while therapists provide clinical intervention designed to create specific changes.

Why Good Intentions Can Backfire

When you try to be your partner's therapist, several problematic dynamics can develop that actually hinder their growth and damage your relationship.

Role confusion issues:

Your partner might become passive: If you take responsibility for their emotional awareness and growth, they don't develop these skills themselves.

Dependency rather than growth: They might begin relying on you for emotional regulation rather than learning to manage their own emotions.

Loss of romantic connection: The relationship becomes more about therapy than love, intimacy, and mutual support.

Resentment on both sides: You might feel frustrated by lack of progress while they feel controlled or pressured to change.

Therapeutic process interference:

Different standards and approaches: Your methods might conflict with professional treatment they're receiving.

Dual relationships create confusion: It's impossible to be both intimate partner and therapeutic guide simultaneously.

Progress resistance: People often resist changing for partners in ways they don't resist changing for neutral professionals.

Shame and pressure: When progress is slow, both people can feel like the relationship itself is failing.

Instead of healing, amateur therapy often creates more stress and distance in the relationship.

Creating Supportive Space Without Managing

Effective support for someone with quiet BPD involves creating emotional space where healing can happen rather than trying to direct the healing process.

The space-holding approach:

Acknowledge without fixing: "I can see you're going through something difficult" without immediately trying to solve or change their experience.

Offer without prescribing: "Is there anything that would help right now?" rather than deciding what they need and providing it.

Listen without analyzing: Hearing their experience without interpreting, explaining, or connecting it to patterns you've observed.

Validate without teaching: Confirming that their feelings make sense without using it as an opportunity to educate about emotions.

Support their choices: Encouraging their autonomy in healing rather than advocating for specific approaches or timelines.

This approach demonstrates love and care while respecting their agency in their own healing process.

Supporting Professional Treatment

When your partner is working with a therapist, your role shifts to supporting their engagement with professional help rather than providing therapy yourself.

Effective support for their therapy:

Practical assistance: Helping with appointment scheduling, transportation, or childcare that makes therapy attendance easier.

Emotional encouragement: Expressing confidence in their ability to grow and change without monitoring their progress.

Reduced pressure at home: Avoiding deep emotional conversations or relationship processing immediately before or after therapy sessions.

Respect for privacy: Not asking detailed questions about therapy content or trying to coordinate with their therapist.

Patience with the process: Understanding that therapy progress is often slow and not always visible in daily life.

What to avoid:

Competing with their therapist: Offering different advice or interpretations of their behavior.

Monitoring their homework: Checking whether they're doing therapeutic assignments or practicing skills.

Discussing their therapy content: Using information they share about therapy in relationship arguments or discussions.

Setting timeline expectations: Pressuring them to make specific progress within certain timeframes.

Becoming their therapy motivator: Taking responsibility for their engagement or attendance rather than letting them manage their own treatment.

Your job is supporting their autonomy in healing, not managing or monitoring their therapeutic process.

Maintaining Your Own Identity and Needs

One of the biggest risks of having a partner with quiet BPD is losing yourself in their emotional world while neglecting your own growth and well-being.

Common ways partners lose themselves:

Emotional absorption: Spending so much energy monitoring your partner's emotions that you lose touch with your own.

Identity merger: Defining yourself primarily as "the partner of someone with BPD" rather than as an individual with your own interests and goals.

Social isolation: Avoiding social connections because you're focused on managing your partner's emotional needs.

Neglected self-care: Putting your own physical and emotional health last while prioritizing your partner's well-being.

Career or hobby neglect: Sacrificing personal goals and interests to accommodate your partner's emotional needs.

Reclaiming your identity:

Regular self-check-ins: Asking yourself "What do I need?" and "How am I feeling?" separate from your partner's emotional state.

Independent relationships: Maintaining friendships and family connections that don't involve your partner.

Personal interests and goals: Pursuing activities, hobbies, and ambitions that are yours alone.

Professional or creative development: Investing in your own growth and skills rather than focusing exclusively on relationship dynamics.

Physical and emotional self-care: Prioritizing your own health and well-being as essential rather than optional.

A healthy relationship requires two whole people, not one person who's lost themselves in caring for another.

Setting Boundaries Around Emotional Labor

Living with someone who has quiet BPD can create enormous emotional labor demands that need clear boundaries to prevent burnout and resentment.

Boundaries around emotional responsibility:

"I care about your emotional well-being, and I'm not responsible for managing your emotions."

"I want to support you, and I also need you to communicate your needs directly rather than expecting me to guess."

"I can offer comfort when you're struggling, and I can't be your primary source of emotional regulation."

"I'm happy to help during difficult times, and I also need to maintain my own emotional health."

Boundaries around problem-solving:

"I can listen when you want to talk about problems, and I won't try to fix everything for you."

"I support your ability to handle your own challenges, with professional help when needed."

"I'm here for emotional support, and I'm not going to become your therapist or life coach."

These boundaries protect your emotional energy while encouraging your partner to develop their own emotional management skills.

A Real-World Role Navigation Story

Consider a physical therapist whose partner worked as a graphic designer. When the designer began experiencing what looked like depression and increased emotional withdrawal, the physical therapist initially responded by trying to help in every way possible.

They researched quiet BPD extensively, learned about emotional regulation techniques, and began trying to guide their partner through mindfulness exercises and emotional awareness practices. They monitored the designer's moods, anticipated their needs, and took responsibility for preventing emotional triggers.

The physical therapist felt like they were being the most supportive partner possible, but several problems developed. The designer became increasingly passive about their own emotional experience, relying on their partner to identify when they were struggling and what might help. The relationship began feeling more like therapy than romance.

The turning point came when the physical therapist realized they were more invested in the designer's emotional growth than the designer was. They were tracking progress, setting goals, and feeling frustrated when improvement was slow - essentially trying to be their partner's therapist while also being their romantic partner.

The physical therapist made a conscious decision to step back from the therapeutic role. Instead of analyzing the designer's emotions, they began simply acknowledging: "I notice you seem quiet today." Instead of prescribing solutions, they started asking: "Is there anything you need from me right now?"

They also began focusing more on their own emotional needs and interests. They reconnected with friends, returned to hobbies they'd neglected, and stopped making their partner's emotional state the center of their attention.

This shift initially felt scary - like they were abandoning their partner during a difficult time. But the result was surprising: the designer began taking more responsibility for their own emotional experience. Without someone else monitoring and managing their emotions, they started noticing their own patterns and needs.

Eventually, the designer sought professional therapy, motivated by their own desire for change rather than their partner's concern about their well-being. The relationship became more balanced, with both people taking responsibility for their own emotional health while supporting each other appropriately.

When Your Partner Resists Professional Help

Sometimes your partner might refuse therapy or insist they can handle their emotional struggles alone. This creates a challenging situation where you want to help but can't force them to seek appropriate treatment.

Effective responses to treatment resistance:

Respect their autonomy: You can't force someone into therapy, and attempting to do so often increases resistance.

Express concern without ultimatums: "I'm worried about you and think talking to someone might help" rather than "You need therapy or I'm leaving."

Focus on relationship impact: Discussing how their emotional unavailability affects the relationship without diagnosing or pathologizing them.

Set boundaries around what you can provide: Being clear about what support you can offer while encouraging professional help for needs you can't meet.

Model help-seeking behavior: Seeking your own therapy or support to demonstrate that professional help is normal and beneficial.

What doesn't work:

Threatening or ultimatums: "Get therapy or I'm leaving" often increases shame and resistance.

Diagnosing or pathologizing: Telling them they have BPD or mental health problems that require treatment.

Researching for them: Finding therapists, making appointments, or managing their treatment process.

Withholding support to force therapy: Using emotional withdrawal as leverage to make them seek help.

You can express concern and set boundaries around what you can provide, but you can't force someone to want professional help.

Building Your Own Support System

Supporting someone with quiet BPD requires your own sources of support, guidance, and emotional refueling.

Professional support options for partners:

Individual therapy: Working with your own therapist to process the challenges of loving someone with quiet BPD.

Support groups: Connecting with other partners of people with BPD (online or in-person groups).

Couples therapy: Working together on relationship dynamics with a therapist who understands quiet BPD.

Educational programs: Attending workshops or classes about BPD and relationship skills.

Personal support network:

Trusted friends: People you can talk to honestly about relationship challenges without judgment.

Family members: Relatives who provide emotional support and perspective on your relationship.

Mentors or advisors: People with wisdom about relationships who can offer guidance and perspective.

Professional colleagues: Work relationships that provide identity and purpose beyond your romantic relationship.

Self-care practices:

Physical health: Exercise, nutrition, sleep, and medical care that maintain your physical well-being.

Mental health: Activities that reduce stress, increase joy, and maintain emotional balance.

Spiritual or philosophical practices: Whatever gives your life meaning and purpose beyond your relationship.

Creative or intellectual pursuits: Activities that engage different parts of your identity and provide fulfillment.

You can't pour from an empty cup - maintaining your own emotional health is essential for being genuinely supportive to your partner.

Recognizing When You Need More Help

Sometimes the challenges of supporting someone with quiet BPD become more than any partner should handle alone.

Signs you need additional support:

Your own mental health is declining: Increased anxiety, depression, or emotional instability that interferes with your daily life.

Social isolation: You've lost touch with friends and family because of relationship demands.

Identity confusion: You're not sure who you are outside of being your partner's support system.

Resentment and burnout: Feeling angry about the emotional labor imbalance or exhausted by constant caregiving.

Enabling patterns: Realizing you're preventing your partner's growth by doing their emotional work for them.

Relationship deterioration: The romantic connection is being overwhelmed by caretaking dynamics.

When these patterns develop, professional help becomes necessary - not just for your partner, but for you and the relationship.

Celebrating Appropriate Support

Learning to support without overstepping isn't about caring less - it's about caring more effectively. When you stop trying to be your partner's therapist, you can return to being their loving partner, which is what they actually need most.

What effective support looks like:

Presence without pressure: Being emotionally available without demanding specific responses or changes.

Encouragement without management: Supporting their growth while respecting their autonomy and timeline.

Love without conditions: Caring about their well-being without making your love dependent on their progress.

Boundaries with compassion: Protecting your own emotional health while remaining open to appropriate connection.

Partnership rather than caretaking: Creating a relationship between two adults rather than one person taking care of another.

This balanced approach creates space for both people to grow, heal, and develop while maintaining genuine intimacy and connection.

Your role in your partner's healing is to love them authentically while encouraging their development of the tools and support they need for genuine growth. You can't heal them, but you can create a relationship environment where healing becomes possible.

This understanding leads us to explore what happens when your support and encouragement aren't enough - when your partner resists change, denies problems, or seems unable to engage in their own healing process despite your best efforts.

Chapter 9: When Love Isn't Enough

You've done everything right. You've learned about quiet BPD, created emotional safety, encouraged professional help, and maintained appropriate boundaries between support and therapy. You've been patient, understanding, and compassionate. Yet your partner continues to insist they're fine, avoids addressing relationship issues, and seems unable or unwilling to engage in any meaningful change process.

This is one of the most heartbreaking aspects of loving someone with quiet BPD: sometimes your love, understanding, and support aren't enough to motivate the growth and healing that's needed for the relationship to thrive. Treatment resistance in quiet BPD often looks different from other forms of avoidance - your partner might agree that therapy could be helpful while never actually engaging, or they might attend sessions without allowing themselves to be vulnerable enough for real change to occur.

Understanding why change feels so threatening to someone with quiet BPD - and what you can and cannot do about their resistance - becomes essential for protecting your own well-being while maintaining appropriate hope for your relationship's future.

Understanding Resistance in Overcontrolled Personalities

For someone with quiet BPD, the very changes that would improve their life and relationships can feel existentially threatening. Their emotional control system developed as protection against perceived dangers, and dismantling that system requires facing the fears that created it in the first place.

Why change feels dangerous:

Loss of emotional control: The rigid emotional management that characterizes quiet BPD provides safety through predictability. Change threatens this sense of control.

Fear of emotional flooding: If they allow themselves to feel emotions more freely, they worry about being overwhelmed by intensity they can't manage.

Identity protection: Their "perfect" or "low-maintenance" identity feels safer than risking being seen as emotional or needy.

Shame about needing help: Seeking therapy or admitting to problems feels like confirmation that they're fundamentally flawed.

Terror of abandonment: They might fear that becoming more emotionally authentic will reveal inadequacies that drive you away.

Previous therapy failures: If therapy hasn't helped before, they might feel hopeless about the possibility of change.

Understanding these fears doesn't excuse indefinite avoidance, but it helps explain why someone might resist change even when they intellectually recognize it would be beneficial.

Common Forms of Treatment Resistance

Resistance in quiet BPD often appears cooperative on the surface while remaining ineffective in practice.

Intellectual compliance without emotional engagement: Your partner might attend therapy sessions, complete homework assignments, and discuss their patterns intellectually while never allowing themselves to actually feel or process emotions.

"I'm fine" resistance: Despite obvious relationship difficulties, they maintain that they don't have significant problems and that any issues are minor or temporary.

Perfectionist therapy performance: They might become the "ideal client" who says the right things and follows all recommendations while keeping their authentic emotional experience completely protected.

Analysis without action: They can discuss their patterns extensively and even understand how they developed without taking any steps toward actual change.

External focus: Redirecting all conversations toward your needs, relationship dynamics, or external stressors while avoiding examination of their internal experience.

Schedule and logistics avoidance: Agreeing to seek help while consistently finding reasons why now isn't the right time - too busy at work, financial concerns, scheduling conflicts.

These forms of resistance can continue indefinitely because they appear to address concerns while avoiding the vulnerability that real change requires.

The Difference Between Can't and Won't

One of the most challenging aspects of treatment resistance is determining whether your partner genuinely can't engage in change (due to trauma, fear, or limited emotional capacity) or won't engage (due to avoidance, denial, or lack of motivation).

Signs of "can't" (limited capacity):

- Genuine confusion about their emotional experience
- Visible distress when attempting emotional expression
- Dissociation or shutdown during emotional conversations
- History of trauma that makes vulnerability feel dangerous
- Clear desire to change but inability to access emotions

Signs of "won't" (avoidance or denial):

- Intellectual understanding without emotional engagement
- Ability to be emotionally expressive in some contexts but not others

- Making excuses for why change isn't necessary or possible

- Refusing to acknowledge relationship problems despite clear evidence

- Prioritizing comfort and control over growth and connection

The distinction matters because limited capacity calls for patience and modified approaches, while persistent avoidance might require clearer boundaries and consequences.

Motivational Strategies That Don't Work

Many traditional approaches to motivating change actually increase resistance in people with quiet BPD.

Ineffective motivational approaches:

Logical arguments about why they should change: Someone with quiet BPD usually understands intellectually that change would be beneficial but feels emotionally unable to risk the vulnerability change requires.

Pointing out relationship problems: Highlighting what's wrong often increases shame and defensiveness rather than motivation for change.

Threats or ultimatums: "Get help or I'm leaving" often triggers abandonment fears that increase emotional shutdown rather than encouraging growth.

Emotional pursuing: Trying to convince them that you won't leave if they become more vulnerable often feels overwhelming rather than reassuring.

Comparison to others: Suggesting they look at how other people handle emotions usually increases feelings of inadequacy rather than motivation.

Timeline pressure: Setting deadlines for change often triggers perfectionism and control needs that make authentic emotional engagement more difficult.

These approaches often backfire because they increase the very fears that created the resistance in the first place.

Working With Resistance Instead of Against It

Rather than trying to overcome resistance, sometimes the most effective approach is acknowledging and working with it while maintaining appropriate boundaries.

Resistance-informed approaches:

Validate the fear behind resistance: "I understand that opening up emotionally feels scary" rather than arguing that they shouldn't be afraid.

Reduce pressure while maintaining boundaries: "I'm not going to pressure you to change, and I also need to take care of my own needs in this relationship."

Focus on small steps: Encouraging tiny changes rather than dramatic emotional breakthroughs.

Respect their timeline while protecting yourself: Allowing them to move at their own pace while setting boundaries around what you can accept long-term.

Address resistance directly: "I notice therapy doesn't seem to be helping much. What's that about?" rather than pretending everything is fine.

This approach honors their autonomy while maintaining realistic expectations about relationship needs.

Setting Boundaries Around Change

While you can't force someone to change, you can set boundaries around what you're willing to accept in a relationship over time.

Healthy boundaries around growth:

"I support your right to seek help or not seek help, and I also need to see some movement toward addressing our relationship issues."

"I'm not going to pressure you to go to therapy, and I also can't pretend that our communication problems aren't affecting my well-being."

"I understand change is difficult, and I need to see that you're actively working on our relationship in some way."

"I respect that you might not be ready for therapy, and I also need you to acknowledge that we have real problems that need attention."

What boundaries are NOT:

- Ultimatums designed to force specific actions
- Threats to leave unless they change immediately
- Conditions that require them to be different than they are
- Attempts to control their choices or timeline

Boundaries protect your well-being while respecting their autonomy, creating space for them to choose change rather than being forced into it.

When Professional Help Becomes Non-Negotiable

Sometimes relationship problems reach a point where professional help isn't just helpful but necessary for the relationship to continue.

Situations requiring professional intervention:

Safety concerns: If you're worried about self-harm, suicide, or other dangerous behaviors, professional help becomes essential regardless of their willingness.

Complete relationship breakdown: When communication has deteriorated so much that you can't address problems together anymore.

Your own mental health decline: If supporting them is causing significant damage to your emotional well-being, professional help for one or both of you becomes necessary.

Patterns that threaten the relationship's survival: When the same problems keep recurring despite multiple attempts to address them together.

Children are being affected: If there are children involved whose well-being is being impacted by relationship dynamics.

In these situations, you might need to make professional help a requirement for the relationship to continue, not as manipulation but as a boundary around what's sustainable for you.

A Real-World Resistance Navigation Story

Consider a teacher whose partner worked in marketing and had struggled with emotional availability throughout their three-year relationship. The teacher had learned about quiet BPD, encouraged therapy, and worked hard to create emotional safety while addressing their own patterns.

The marketing professional agreed that therapy might be helpful and found a therapist they liked. They attended sessions regularly for six months, did homework assignments, and could discuss their patterns intellectually. However, no actual changes occurred in their emotional availability or relationship communication.

The marketing professional would say things like "My therapist and I are working on my tendency to withdraw when stressed" while continuing to withdraw whenever stress occurred. They could explain their attachment patterns and childhood influences while remaining completely disconnected from their emotions.

The teacher initially felt hopeful about the therapy engagement and tried to be patient with the slow progress. However, after months of intellectual therapy without emotional change, they realized their partner was performing therapy rather than actually engaging in it.

The breakthrough conversation happened when the teacher said: "I'm concerned that you're going through the motions of therapy without allowing yourself to be vulnerable enough for real change. I'm not going to tell you how to do therapy, but I need to see some actual movement in our relationship dynamic."

This conversation led to a difficult but honest discussion about how therapy had become another way for the marketing professional to avoid real emotional engagement - they could feel good about "working on themselves" without actually risking vulnerability.

The marketing professional eventually acknowledged that they'd been treating therapy like a performance, saying what they thought their therapist wanted to hear while keeping their authentic emotional experience completely protected. This recognition became the beginning of more genuine engagement with their therapeutic process.

The change wasn't dramatic or immediate, but it was real. The marketing professional began taking emotional risks in therapy first, then gradually in their relationship. They learned that vulnerability didn't automatically lead to rejection and that authentic connection felt better than perfect performance.

Alternative Approaches When Traditional Therapy Fails

Sometimes standard therapy approaches don't work for people with quiet BPD, requiring creative alternatives or different therapeutic modalities.

Alternative healing approaches:

Group therapy or support groups: Sometimes hearing from others with similar struggles reduces isolation and shame more effectively than individual therapy.

Experiential therapies: Art therapy, music therapy, or movement therapy might access emotions that talk therapy can't reach.

Intensive programs: Retreat-style programs or intensive outpatient treatment might create breakthroughs that weekly therapy sessions can't achieve.

Somatic or body-based approaches: Therapies that work with physical sensations and body awareness rather than cognitive processing.

Couples therapy as an entry point: Some people can engage emotionally in couples therapy when individual therapy feels too threatening.

Peer support or coaching: Sometimes non-clinical support feels safer than traditional therapy relationships.

The key is finding approaches that feel safe enough for your partner to engage authentically rather than continuing ineffective treatment because it seems like the "right" thing to do.

Accepting Limitations

One of the hardest realizations in relationships with treatment-resistant quiet BPD is that you might need to accept limitations in what's possible for your relationship.

What acceptance might look like:

Recognizing that your partner might never be emotionally available in the ways you need

Understanding that change might be so slow that it doesn't meaningfully impact your relationship

Accepting that their emotional capacity might be genuinely limited rather than just temporarily restricted

Realizing that your love and support, while valuable, aren't enough to overcome years of emotional protection patterns

Acknowledging that you might need to choose between staying in a limited relationship or leaving to find deeper emotional connection

Acceptance doesn't mean giving up hope, but it does mean making decisions based on current reality rather than potential future change.

Making Difficult Decisions

When resistance to change continues despite your best efforts, you might face difficult decisions about your relationship's future.

Factors to consider:

Quality of life: How is the relationship affecting your daily emotional well-being, stress levels, and life satisfaction?

Future prospects: Based on current patterns, what does the next five or ten years likely look like?

Your own growth: Are you able to continue developing and pursuing your goals within this relationship?

Children's well-being: If children are involved, how are relationship dynamics affecting their emotional development?

Alternative possibilities: What kind of relationship and emotional connection might be possible with a different partner?

Your partner's potential: Do you see genuine signs that change is possible, or are you hoping for changes that might never occur?

These decisions aren't about whether your partner is a good person or whether you love them - they're about whether the relationship can meet your fundamental emotional needs.

When Leaving Becomes Necessary

Sometimes the most loving thing you can do for both yourself and your partner is end a relationship that isn't working despite everyone's best efforts.

Signs that ending the relationship might be necessary:

Your mental health is seriously declining despite professional support

Years of effort haven't produced meaningful changes in relationship dynamics

You've lost touch with who you are outside of managing this relationship

Your partner shows no genuine motivation to address relationship problems

You're staying only out of guilt, fear, or hope for future change rather than current relationship satisfaction

Children are being negatively affected by relationship dynamics

Leaving doesn't mean you failed or didn't love enough - sometimes it means recognizing that love alone isn't sufficient for a healthy relationship.

Finding Peace With Uncertainty

Whether you stay or leave, relationships involving treatment-resistant quiet BPD often require learning to live with uncertainty about the future.

Making peace with uncertainty:

Focus on what you can control: Your own choices, boundaries, and emotional well-being rather than your partner's willingness to change.

Find meaning beyond the relationship: Develop sources of purpose, joy, and fulfillment that don't depend on relationship dynamics.

Accept that some questions don't have answers: You might never know why your partner can't or won't change, and that's okay.

Trust your own judgment: You're the expert on what you can and cannot accept in a relationship long-term.

Seek support for your decisions: Whatever you choose, make sure you have people who support your autonomy and well-being.

Love is essential but not sufficient for healthy relationships. When love isn't enough to motivate necessary changes, you're not failing - you're facing one of the most difficult realities of human relationships.

The wisdom gained from grappling with treatment resistance prepares you for the next phase of your journey - whether that involves rebuilding intimacy in your current relationship or finding the courage to seek the emotional connection you deserve elsewhere.

These principles direct our attention to how couples can work together when both people are committed to growth, and what becomes possible when emotional walls finally begin to come down.

Chapter 10: Intimacy Without Invasion

Rebuilding intimacy in a quiet BPD relationship feels like learning to dance with someone who's forgotten how to move to music. The desire for connection exists on both sides, but the skills and safety needed for authentic emotional intimacy have been buried under years of protective patterns. You want to get closer, but every step toward genuine vulnerability seems to trigger withdrawal. Your partner craves connection but experiences emotional intimacy as threatening rather than nourishing.

Creating true intimacy requires dismantling walls that were built for protection while ensuring your partner feels safe enough to risk emotional vulnerability. This isn't about forcing connection or breaking down defenses - it's about creating conditions where authentic sharing becomes possible gradually and naturally.

The goal isn't to eliminate all emotional protection but to develop flexibility around when walls are needed and when they can safely come down.

Understanding Intimacy Versus Invasion

For someone with quiet BPD, the line between intimate connection and emotional invasion can be impossibly thin. What feels like loving closeness to you might feel overwhelming or threatening to them, triggering their protective systems and causing withdrawal just when connection seems most possible.

What intimacy looks like:

- Mutual emotional sharing that respects both people's capacity
- Vulnerability that's offered freely rather than demanded or pursued

- Connection that enhances both people's sense of self rather than threatening individual identity
- Emotional exchange that feels safe and nourishing rather than overwhelming
- Closeness that can be adjusted based on current emotional capacity

What invasion feels like:

- Pressure to share more than feels emotionally safe
- Questions or conversations that feel like emotional demands
- Closeness that requires sacrificing emotional protection before feeling ready
- Vulnerability that feels forced or manipulated rather than chosen
- Connection that threatens their sense of control or autonomy

Learning to distinguish between these experiences helps you offer genuine intimacy without accidentally creating emotional invasion.

Creating Safety for Emotional Expression

Safety isn't just the absence of criticism or rejection - for someone with quiet BPD, emotional safety requires specific conditions that make vulnerability feel possible rather than dangerous.

Elements of emotional safety:

Predictable responses: Your partner needs to know that emotional sharing won't result in dramatic reactions, immediate problem-solving attempts, or pressure for more disclosure.

Respect for timing: Safety includes the right to share emotions when ready rather than when requested or demanded.

Non-judgmental reception: Emotional expressions need to be received without analysis, interpretation, or suggestions for change.

Maintained autonomy: Your partner needs to know that sharing emotions won't result in loss of independence or being treated as fragile.

Permission to retreat: Safety includes the right to return to emotional protection after moments of vulnerability without it being seen as rejection.

How to create safety:

Respond to emotional sharing with simple acknowledgment: "Thank you for telling me that" rather than immediate comfort, advice, or questions.

Avoid pursuing when they share something vulnerable: Resist the urge to ask follow-up questions or push for more details when they offer emotional information.

Don't treat emotional expression as crisis: Respond to their feelings as normal human experience rather than problems that need immediate attention.

Maintain consistent behavior regardless of their emotional state: Don't dramatically change how you interact with them based on what they share.

Express appreciation without pressure: Acknowledge when they share emotions without making it about your need for more connection.

Graduated Emotional Exposure

Rather than expecting your partner to suddenly become emotionally open, intimacy develops through gradual exposure to emotional expression and connection.

Starting with low-risk emotional sharing:

Daily experience emotions: Feelings about work, weather, food, or activities that don't involve deep vulnerability.

Appreciation and gratitude: Sharing positive feelings that don't require reciprocation or deep emotional processing.

Preferences and opinions: Emotional reactions to movies, books, or current events that feel safer than personal emotions.

Past experiences without trauma: Sharing feelings about neutral memories or experiences that don't involve pain or vulnerability.

Gradually increasing emotional depth:

Current stress without crisis: Sharing manageable work or life pressures that don't require problem-solving.

Relationship appreciation: Expressing positive feelings about your connection without demands for reciprocation.

Mild disappointments or frustrations: Sharing manageable negative emotions about external situations.

Personal fears or hopes: Eventually sharing more vulnerable emotions about future goals or concerns.

The key is allowing your partner to control the pace and depth of emotional sharing rather than pushing for faster or deeper connection.

Building Secure Attachment Patterns

Quiet BPD often involves insecure attachment patterns where closeness triggers fears of abandonment or engulfment. Building secure attachment requires consistent experiences that connection enhances rather than threatens individual well-being.

Secure attachment behaviors:

Consistent availability without pursuit: Being emotionally present when your partner seeks connection without chasing them when they withdraw.

Reliable responses to emotional needs: Responding predictably and helpfully when your partner directly expresses needs.

Respect for independence: Supporting your partner's autonomy and individual interests rather than trying to merge identities.

Emotional regulation: Managing your own emotions rather than expecting your partner to provide constant reassurance or emotional management.

Trustworthy communication: Following through on commitments and being honest about your own emotional experience.

Healing insecure attachment:

Demonstrating that connection doesn't equal loss of self: Showing that emotional intimacy can coexist with individual identity and autonomy.

Proving that vulnerability doesn't lead to abandonment: Consistently responding with care rather than rejection when your partner shares difficult emotions.

Showing that closeness doesn't require perfection: Accepting your partner's full emotional range rather than only supporting positive emotions.

Modeling healthy emotional boundaries: Demonstrating that people can be close while maintaining individual emotional responsibility.

Physical and Emotional Intimacy Balance

Physical intimacy and emotional intimacy often become disconnected in quiet BPD relationships, with physical connection sometimes substituting for emotional sharing.

Reconnecting physical and emotional intimacy:

Emotional check-ins during physical connection: Asking "How are you feeling right now?" during intimate moments without requiring detailed answers.

Physical comfort during emotional sharing: Offering appropriate physical touch when your partner shares emotions, if they're receptive.

Presence without performance: Being physically close without demands for specific emotional or sexual responses.

Synchronized emotional and physical connection: Gradually learning to share emotions and physical affection simultaneously rather than keeping them separate.

Avoiding physical intimacy as emotional bypass:

Don't use physical connection to avoid difficult conversations: Address relationship issues directly rather than hoping physical intimacy will resolve emotional disconnection.

Respect when physical and emotional availability don't match: Understanding that your partner might need physical space during emotional processing or vice versa.

Avoid pressuring for physical connection when emotional connection feels unsafe: Allow both types of intimacy to develop at their own pace.

Trust Rebuilding After Withdrawal Cycles

Repeated cycles of connection followed by withdrawal can damage trust and make both people hesitant to invest emotionally in the relationship.

Rebuilding trust requires:

Acknowledging the impact of withdrawal patterns: Recognizing that emotional unavailability affects the relationship even when it's not intentional.

Understanding rather than eliminating withdrawal: Working to understand withdrawal triggers rather than demanding that withdrawal never happen.

Creating predictability around emotional cycles: Developing awareness of patterns so both people can prepare for and navigate difficult periods.

Rebuilding faith in connection: Gradually demonstrating that emotional intimacy can be sustained rather than inevitably leading to withdrawal.

For the partner with quiet BPD:

- Learning to recognize early warning signs of emotional overwhelm

- Developing communication tools for managing withdrawal needs

- Building tolerance for sustained emotional connection

- Practicing repair attempts after withdrawal periods

For the supporting partner:

- Learning not to take withdrawal personally while acknowledging its impact

- Developing patience for the gradual nature of trust rebuilding

- Maintaining emotional availability without pursuing during withdrawal

- Focusing on long-term patterns rather than individual incidents

A Real-World Intimacy Building Journey

Consider a nurse whose partner worked as an engineer. After learning about quiet BPD and working on communication patterns, they wanted to rebuild emotional intimacy that had been missing from their relationship for years.

The engineer had learned to share basic emotions and communicate needs more directly, but deeper emotional intimacy still felt threatening. They could discuss work stress or daily frustrations but withdrew whenever conversations touched on their relationship, childhood, or future hopes and fears.

The nurse initially tried to encourage deeper sharing by asking thoughtful questions and creating special time for intimate conversations. However, these efforts often led to the engineer becoming overwhelmed and withdrawn, creating more distance rather than increased connection.

The breakthrough came when the nurse shifted from pursuing emotional intimacy to creating space where it could naturally develop. Instead of asking about deep emotions, they began sharing their own feelings without expecting reciprocation.

They started with low-risk emotional sharing: "I'm feeling grateful for this quiet evening together" or "I was thinking today about how much I enjoy our weekend routine." They expressed appreciation for small moments without making them into big emotional conversations.

Over time, the engineer began responding to these small emotional offerings with their own brief emotional expressions. They might say "I feel peaceful when we're like this" or "I was happy when you laughed at that movie scene."

The nurse learned to receive these small emotional gifts without immediately building on them or asking for more. They would simply acknowledge: "I'm glad you shared that with me" and allow the moment to exist without pressure for expansion.

Gradually, the engineer's capacity for emotional sharing grew. They began mentioning feelings about work relationships, expressing appreciation for things the nurse did, and occasionally sharing concerns about family or future plans.

The key was allowing intimacy to develop organically rather than trying to create it through direct pursuit. When emotional sharing felt optional rather than required, the engineer felt safe enough to gradually offer more authentic connection.

After months of this patient approach, they were able to have conversations about their relationship, their individual growth, and their shared hopes for the future - conversations that would have been impossible when emotional intimacy felt like emotional invasion.

Creating Connection Rituals

Developing regular practices that create opportunities for connection without pressure can help rebuild intimacy gradually and sustainably.

Low-pressure connection rituals:

Daily appreciation sharing: Each person shares one thing they appreciated about the other that day, without discussion or reciprocal requirements.

Weekly check-ins: Regular time to discuss practical matters and general well-being without pressure for deep emotional processing.

Shared activities without performance pressure: Cooking together, taking walks, or engaging in hobbies side by side without requiring conversation or emotional exchange.

Bedtime gratitude: Sharing one positive thing from the day before sleep, creating positive association with vulnerable moments.

Physical affection without sexual pressure: Regular non-sexual touch like hand-holding, hugs, or sitting close while watching television.

Higher-intimacy rituals for when ready:

Monthly relationship meetings: Structured time to discuss relationship dynamics, appreciation, and concerns when both people feel emotionally ready.

Shared goal setting: Discussing future hopes and plans together when your partner feels safe sharing vulnerable aspirations.

Emotional processing time: Designated periods for deeper emotional conversation when your partner initiates or specifically agrees to such discussions.

Conflict resolution practices: Structured approaches to addressing disagreements when both people feel capable of emotional engagement.

The key is establishing these rituals based on current emotional capacity rather than ideal relationship goals, allowing them to deepen naturally over time.

Managing Expectations and Celebrating Progress

Rebuilding intimacy in quiet BPD relationships requires adjusting expectations to match realistic timelines and recognizing subtle progress that might be invisible to outside observers.

Realistic expectations for intimacy rebuilding:

Progress is measured in months and years, not days or weeks

Emotional intimacy might always require more conscious effort than in other relationships

Some level of emotional protection might always be necessary for your partner's well-being

Intimacy might look different from cultural ideals while still being genuine and satisfying

Setbacks and withdrawal periods are part of the process rather than signs of failure

Celebrating meaningful progress:

Your partner sharing any emotion directly rather than expecting you to guess

Increased comfort with your emotional expression without withdrawal

Longer periods between emotional shutdown cycles

More frequent initiation of physical or emotional connection

Willingness to discuss relationship dynamics without defensiveness

Ability to stay present during conflict rather than immediately withdrawing

Expressions of appreciation or affection that feel spontaneous rather than obligated

Recognizing these subtle improvements helps maintain motivation for the long-term work of rebuilding intimacy.

Creating Your Intimacy Rebuilding Plan

Assessment of current intimacy capacity:

What level of emotional sharing feels safe for your partner right now?

What types of physical connection are comfortable and desired?

How much emotional processing can your relationship handle without triggering withdrawal?

What past attempts at intimacy have been successful versus overwhelming?

What are your own intimacy needs that feel non-negotiable versus flexible?

Graduated intimacy goals:

Immediate goals (next 1-3 months): Focus on basic emotional safety and small increases in sharing

Medium-term goals (3-6 months): Build capacity for sustained emotional conversation and physical affection

Long-term goals (6+ months): Develop ability to navigate conflict intimately and share vulnerable emotions

Ongoing maintenance: Create sustainable intimacy practices that honor both people's needs and capacity

Support systems for intimacy rebuilding:

Professional guidance: Couples therapy or individual therapy to support the intimacy rebuilding process

Educational resources: Books, workshops, or courses about attachment and emotional intimacy

Peer support: Connections with other couples who understand the unique challenges of quiet BPD relationships

Personal support networks: Individual friendships and family relationships that provide emotional fulfillment beyond the romantic relationship

When Intimacy Rebuilding Stalls

Sometimes despite best efforts, emotional intimacy remains limited or progress stops entirely.

Common obstacles to intimacy rebuilding:

Unaddressed trauma that makes vulnerability feel dangerous

Medication or mental health issues that affect emotional capacity

External stressors that overwhelm emotional resources

Lack of individual therapy or personal growth work

Unrealistic timeline expectations creating pressure and withdrawal

Secondary relationship problems that interfere with intimacy building

Addressing intimacy obstacles:

Professional assessment of barriers: Working with therapists to identify what's preventing emotional connection

Individual therapy for both partners: Addressing personal obstacles to intimacy separately before working on them together

Medical evaluation: Ensuring that physical or mental health issues aren't interfering with emotional capacity

Stress reduction: Addressing external pressures that might be overwhelming emotional resources

Timeline adjustment: Extending expectations and reducing pressure around intimacy development

Alternative approaches: Exploring different ways of creating connection that match your partner's current capacity

The Rewards of Patient Intimacy Building

When emotional intimacy develops gradually and safely, it often becomes stronger and more sustainable than forced or pressured connection.

Benefits of gradual intimacy rebuilding:

Authentic connection: Your partner learns to share their real emotional experience rather than performing intimacy

Sustainable vulnerability: Emotional expression becomes a choice rather than a requirement, making it more likely to continue

Increased relationship satisfaction: Both people feel seen and understood rather than managed or controlled

Better conflict resolution: Ability to address problems emotionally rather than just intellectually

Enhanced individual growth: Both people develop better emotional awareness and expression skills

Deeper trust: Confidence that emotional sharing will be received well and that withdrawal won't mean abandonment

Genuine appreciation: Recognition of the courage required for emotional vulnerability, making connection feel more precious

Rebuilding intimacy after years of emotional protection requires patience, skill, and commitment from both people. When it works, the result is often a deeper and more authentic connection than either person has experienced before.

This foundation enables us to examine the often-overlooked challenge of maintaining your own emotional health while supporting someone through their healing journey - and why your well-being matters for the relationship's success.

Chapter 11: The Caregiver's Survival Guide

Supporting someone with quiet BPD can gradually transform you from a romantic partner into an emotional caregiver without you even realizing it's happening. You become expert at reading subtle mood changes, managing household stress levels, and anticipating needs that are never directly expressed. You pride yourself on being supportive, understanding, and patient. What you might not notice is how this constant emotional labor is affecting your own mental health, social connections, and sense of self.

The research on partners of people with personality disorders reveals a sobering reality: the stress of these relationships can create measurable changes in your nervous system, sleep patterns, and immune function. You're not just imagining that this relationship feels more challenging than others - it actually requires more emotional resources and creates more psychological stress than typical romantic partnerships.

Understanding how to protect your mental health isn't selfish or unsupportive - it's essential for your own well-being and for your ability to maintain a healthy relationship over time.

Recognizing Compassion Fatigue

Compassion fatigue develops when you consistently give more emotional energy than you receive, gradually depleting your capacity for empathy and care. In quiet BPD relationships, this often happens slowly and subtly.

Early signs of compassion fatigue:

Emotional numbing: Finding yourself less responsive to your partner's emotions or feeling disconnected from your own feelings.

Increased irritability: Becoming more easily frustrated with your partner or other people, especially around emotional needs.

Difficulty maintaining boundaries: Finding it harder to distinguish between your emotions and your partner's, or taking responsibility for feelings that aren't yours.

Reduced empathy for others: Having less emotional availability for friends, family, or colleagues because your empathy reserves are depleted.

Physical symptoms: Experiencing headaches, sleep problems, digestive issues, or other stress-related physical symptoms.

Advanced compassion fatigue symptoms:

Emotional exhaustion: Feeling drained even after rest or time away from your partner.

Cynicism about relationships: Beginning to doubt whether healthy relationships are possible or whether people can really change.

Identity confusion: Losing touch with who you are outside of your caregiving role.

Resentment and blame: Feeling angry about the emotional labor imbalance while also feeling guilty about having these feelings.

Avoidance behaviors: Withdrawing from social connections or activities that used to bring joy.

Recognizing these symptoms early allows you to take protective action before compassion fatigue becomes more severe.

Understanding Secondary Trauma

Living with someone who has quiet BPD often means being exposed to their internal emotional pain, even when it's not directly expressed. This secondary exposure to trauma and distress can create its own psychological impact.

How secondary trauma develops:

Emotional absorption: Picking up on your partner's internal distress and carrying it as your own emotional burden.

Hypervigilance: Developing constant alertness to potential emotional crises or problems that need management.

Trauma witness stress: Being aware of your partner's pain while feeling helpless to provide meaningful relief.

Chronic stress activation: Living in a state of low-level emergency readiness due to unpredictable emotional dynamics.

Signs of secondary trauma:

Intrusive thoughts about your partner's well-being: Worrying excessively about their emotional state even when you're apart.

Sleep disturbances: Difficulty falling asleep or staying asleep due to relationship anxiety.

Anxiety symptoms: Physical symptoms like rapid heartbeat, shallow breathing, or muscle tension related to relationship stress.

Avoidance of potential triggers: Changing your behavior to prevent situations that might upset your partner.

Emotional flashbacks: Re-experiencing the stress of past relationship crises or conflicts.

Loss of safety perception: Feeling like emotional crisis could happen at any time, making relaxation difficult.

Understanding secondary trauma helps you recognize that your stress responses are normal reactions to abnormal relationship dynamics.

Building Your Support Network

One of the most important protective factors for mental health in challenging relationships is maintaining strong connections outside the relationship.

Essential support network elements:

Close friends who understand your situation: People you can talk to honestly about relationship challenges without judgment.

Family members who provide perspective: Relatives who can remind you of your identity outside the relationship.

Professional support: Therapist, counselor, or support group facilitator who understands partner dynamics in personality disorder relationships.

Peer connections: Other partners of people with BPD who can provide specific understanding and validation.

Mentors or advisors: People with wisdom about relationships who can offer guidance and perspective.

Maintaining support networks:

Regular one-on-one time with friends: Scheduling individual connections rather than only socializing as a couple.

Family relationships independent of your partner: Maintaining connections with relatives that don't always include your partner.

Professional relationships: Work or volunteer connections that provide identity and purpose beyond your romantic relationship.

Interest-based communities: Groups organized around hobbies, sports, or activities that give you individual identity.

Online communities: Forums or social media groups where you can connect with others who understand your specific challenges.

The key is maintaining relationships where you can be authentic about your experience rather than having to manage others' perceptions of your partner or relationship.

Professional Help for Partners

Individual therapy for partners isn't just helpful - it's often essential for maintaining mental health while supporting someone with quiet BPD.

What partner therapy can address:

Processing relationship stress: Working through the emotional impact of living with invisible emotional dynamics.

Boundary development: Learning to distinguish between support and enabling, care and codependency.

Identity preservation: Maintaining sense of self while being in a relationship that requires significant emotional accommodation.

Trauma processing: Addressing secondary trauma symptoms and developing resilience.

Communication skills: Learning effective ways to interact with someone who has difficulty expressing emotions.

Decision-making support: Having a safe space to explore options and make decisions about your relationship's future.

Types of therapy that help partners:

Individual therapy focused on relationship stress: Working with therapists who understand personality disorder dynamics.

Cognitive-behavioral therapy: Learning to recognize and change thought patterns that increase relationship stress.

Trauma-informed therapy: Addressing secondary trauma and developing resilience.

Support groups for BPD partners: Connecting with others who face similar challenges.

Couples therapy: Working together on relationship dynamics when both people are willing and able.

Don't wait until you're in crisis to seek professional support - preventive therapy can help you develop skills before problems become overwhelming.

Self-Care as Survival Strategy

Self-care in challenging relationships isn't luxury - it's a survival strategy that maintains your capacity to function and make healthy decisions.

Physical self-care priorities:

Sleep hygiene: Protecting your sleep despite relationship stress through consistent routines and anxiety management.

Regular exercise: Physical activity that helps process stress and maintain emotional regulation.

Nutrition support: Eating regularly and healthily even when relationship stress affects appetite.

Medical care: Staying current with healthcare and addressing stress-related physical symptoms.

Substance awareness: Monitoring alcohol or other substance use that might increase due to relationship stress.

Emotional self-care practices:

Daily emotional check-ins: Regular assessment of your own feelings separate from your partner's emotional state.

Stress management techniques: Meditation, breathing exercises, or other practices that help regulate your nervous system.

Creative expression: Activities that allow emotional processing and provide joy beyond relationship dynamics.

Spiritual or philosophical practices: Whatever gives your life meaning and perspective beyond your romantic relationship.

Professional emotional support: Therapy, counseling, or coaching that focuses on your individual well-being.

Social self-care maintenance:

Friend time that doesn't involve relationship discussion: Social connections that allow you to be yourself rather than a support-seeking partner.

Family relationships: Maintaining connections with relatives who knew you before this relationship.

New social opportunities: Trying new activities or groups that expand your social circle.

Boundary setting around support requests: Learning to ask for help for your own needs rather than always being the helper.

A Real-World Caregiver Recovery Story

Consider a social worker whose partner had quiet BPD. The social worker's professional training made them highly attuned to emotional needs and skilled at providing support, which initially felt helpful in their relationship.

Over two years, the social worker gradually took on more emotional responsibility - monitoring their partner's moods, managing household stress, and providing constant emotional support while receiving little reciprocation. They prided themselves on being understanding and patient.

However, the social worker began experiencing symptoms they didn't recognize: difficulty sleeping, increased anxiety at work, and emotional exhaustion that rest didn't relieve. They found themselves less available to friends and family, declining social invitations to be available for their partner's needs.

The wake-up call came during a routine medical appointment when their doctor expressed concern about elevated blood pressure and suggested stress management. The social worker realized they'd been so focused on their partner's emotional health that they'd ignored their own physical stress symptoms.

They began individual therapy focused on partner self-care and boundary development. Through this work, they recognized how their professional helping skills had become overextended in their personal relationship, creating an unhealthy dynamic where they felt responsible for their partner's emotional well-being.

The recovery process involved gradually redistributing emotional labor in the relationship. The social worker learned to express their own needs directly, set boundaries around emotional availability, and maintain individual interests and friendships.

They also developed stress management practices specifically designed for relationship stress: regular exercise that served as emotional reset time, weekly individual therapy sessions, and monthly weekend trips with friends that provided perspective and renewal.

The changes weren't easy - their partner initially struggled with the reduced emotional caretaking. However, over time, both people benefited from a more balanced dynamic where both individuals took responsibility for their own emotional well-being while supporting each other appropriately.

The social worker learned that protecting their own mental health wasn't selfish - it was essential for maintaining their capacity to love and support their partner sustainably over time.

Managing Emotional Absorption

One of the biggest challenges for partners is learning to care about your partner's emotional experience without absorbing it as your own.

Emotional boundary techniques:

Daily emotional separation practice: Regularly asking yourself "What am I feeling versus what is my partner feeling?"

Physical space for emotional processing: Having a physical location where you can process your own emotions separately.

Emotional temperature checks: Before and after time with your partner, assessing your own emotional state.

Energy protection visualization: Imagining emotional barriers that allow care to flow out while preventing absorption of your partner's emotions.

Response versus reaction training: Learning to respond to your partner's emotions thoughtfully rather than automatically reacting.

Distinguishing care from absorption:

Caring looks like: "I can see you're struggling and I want to support you."

Absorption looks like: "I feel terrible because you're struggling and I need to fix this."

Caring maintains boundaries: "I'm here for you and I also need to take care of my own emotional needs."

Absorption eliminates boundaries: "Your emotional well-being is more important than mine."

Caring preserves individual identity: "I love you and I am still my own person with my own needs."

Absorption merges identity: "I can't be okay unless you're okay."

Learning this distinction allows you to remain supportive without losing yourself in your partner's emotional experience.

Creating Mental Health Boundaries

Protecting your mental health requires specific boundaries around what you will and won't take responsibility for in the relationship.

Mental health boundary examples:

"I care about your emotional well-being and I'm not responsible for managing your emotions."

"I want to support you through difficult times and I also need to maintain my own emotional health."

"I'm available for reasonable emotional support and I can't be your only source of emotional regulation."

"I love you and I won't sacrifice my mental health to accommodate your emotional needs."

"I'm committed to this relationship and I'm also committed to my own well-being."

Implementing mental health boundaries:

Start with small boundaries: Begin with minor adjustments rather than dramatic changes to relationship dynamics.

Communicate boundaries clearly: Explain your needs and limits directly rather than expecting your partner to guess.

Maintain consistency: Follow through on boundaries even when it feels difficult or creates temporary relationship tension.

Seek support for boundary maintenance: Use therapy or trusted friends to help you maintain boundaries when they feel challenging.

Adjust boundaries as needed: Modify your limits based on what actually protects your mental health rather than theoretical ideals.

Remember that boundaries protect relationships by ensuring both people remain emotionally healthy enough to participate in love and support.

Warning Signs You Need More Support

Certain symptoms indicate that relationship stress is exceeding your capacity to cope and professional help is necessary.

Immediate professional help indicators:

Persistent sleep problems that affect daily functioning

Anxiety or depression symptoms that interfere with work or other relationships

Physical symptoms like chronic headaches, digestive problems, or immune system issues

Substance use increases to cope with relationship stress

Suicidal thoughts or feelings that life isn't worth living

Complete social isolation or loss of interest in activities you previously enjoyed

Inability to function normally in daily responsibilities

Medium-term support needs:

Feeling emotionally exhausted despite rest and self-care efforts

Difficulty maintaining other relationships due to relationship stress

Identity confusion or loss of sense of self outside the relationship

Persistent resentment or anger about relationship dynamics

Considering ending the relationship but feeling unable to make a decision

Recurring conflicts about emotional needs that don't improve over time

Don't wait until you're in crisis to seek help - early intervention is more effective and less disruptive than crisis management.

Building Resilience for the Long Term

Developing resilience helps you maintain emotional health while navigating ongoing relationship challenges.

Resilience building practices:

Regular stress management: Daily practices that help your nervous system recover from relationship stress.

Perspective maintenance: Regular reminders of your life purpose and identity beyond your relationship.

Skill development: Learning communication, boundary-setting, and emotional regulation skills that improve your capacity to handle challenges.

Support network maintenance: Consistently investing in relationships that provide emotional nourishment and perspective.

Professional development: Pursuing goals and interests that give you identity and purpose outside your relationship.

Physical health priority: Maintaining exercise, nutrition, and medical care that support your overall resilience.

Creating sustainable support patterns:

Regular individual therapy: Ongoing professional support rather than only crisis intervention.

Weekly friend or family time: Consistent social connections that provide perspective and emotional refueling.

Monthly individual activities: Pursuing interests or goals that remind you of your individual identity.

Annual relationship assessment: Honest evaluation of whether the relationship is supporting or undermining your overall well-being.

Building resilience allows you to love and support your partner from a position of strength rather than depletion.

When Self-Care Isn't Enough

Sometimes despite excellent self-care and professional support, the relationship stress exceeds what any individual can healthily manage.

Signs that relationship stress is too high:

Self-care efforts aren't preventing mental health decline

Professional support isn't sufficient to manage relationship stress

Physical health problems develop or worsen despite stress management efforts

You've lost touch with who you are outside the relationship despite individual therapy

Other important relationships are suffering despite boundary efforts

You're unable to enjoy life or pursue personal goals despite support and self-care

When self-care isn't enough, the relationship itself might need to change or end for your mental health to recover.

Protecting your mental health isn't just about surviving your current relationship - it's about maintaining your capacity for love, joy, and connection throughout your entire life. You can't pour from an empty cup, and you can't love authentically from a depleted emotional state.

Your well-being matters not just for you but for your ability to be a genuine partner in whatever relationship you choose to build.

As we turn to the next area of exploration, we'll examine the difficult decisions about your relationship's future when love alone isn't sufficient to create the emotional connection both people deserve.

Chapter 12: Staying, Leaving, Or Redefining

You've done the work. You understand quiet BPD, have improved communication patterns, set healthy boundaries, and protected your mental health. You've encouraged professional help and created conditions for emotional growth. Yet you're still facing a fundamental question: Is this relationship capable of meeting your long-term emotional needs, or is it time to consider a different future?

This isn't a question about whether you love your partner or whether they're a good person. It's not about whether you've tried hard enough or whether you're being unreasonable in your expectations. It's about honestly assessing whether the relationship as it exists - or as it's likely to develop - can provide the emotional connection and satisfaction both people deserve.

Sometimes love is enough to sustain a relationship through its challenges and limitations. Sometimes love is present but insufficient to create the intimacy and partnership that healthy relationships require. Learning to distinguish between these situations is one of the most difficult but important skills in adult relationships.

Assessing Progress Versus Hope

After months or years of working on quiet BPD dynamics, it's crucial to distinguish between actual progress and hopeful expectations about future change.

Signs of genuine progress:

Increased emotional expression: Your partner shares feelings more directly and frequently, even if it's still limited compared to typical relationships.

Better conflict resolution: Disagreements can be discussed and resolved rather than triggering withdrawal or shutdown.

Reduced emotional labor imbalance: Your partner takes more responsibility for their emotional awareness and regulation.

Improved response to your emotional needs: When you express needs directly, your partner responds supportively rather than becoming overwhelmed.

Professional help engagement: Your partner actively participates in therapy or other growth work rather than going through the motions.

Decreased withdrawal cycles: Emotional shutdown periods become less frequent, shorter, or less severe over time.

Signs of stagnation despite effort:

No change in emotional availability despite months of work: Your partner remains as emotionally distant as when you started addressing the issues.

Therapy compliance without engagement: They attend sessions or read books but show no actual changes in emotional expression or relationship dynamics.

Intellectual understanding without behavioral change: They can discuss their patterns but continue the same behaviors indefinitely.

Promises of change without follow-through: Expressing intention to be more emotionally available while making no concrete steps toward that goal.

Crisis cycles without learning: The same emotional shutdown or withdrawal patterns repeat without any apparent insight or growth.

Honest assessment requires looking at actual changes over time rather than focusing on potential or intentions.

The Different Types of Relationship Futures

Not all relationship decisions are binary choices between staying exactly as things are or ending the relationship completely.

Staying with accepted limitations: Choosing to remain in the relationship while accepting that emotional intimacy will always be more limited than in typical relationships. This works when both people find sufficient satisfaction and connection within those limitations.

Staying with modified expectations: Remaining together while significantly adjusting relationship expectations to match your partner's emotional capacity. This might mean finding emotional fulfillment through friendships, individual pursuits, or other relationships while maintaining romantic partnership.

Staying with specific conditions: Continuing the relationship contingent on certain changes or commitments, such as ongoing therapy engagement, specific behavioral changes, or timeline agreements for emotional progress.

Redefining the relationship structure: Creating alternative relationship arrangements that better accommodate both people's needs - perhaps reduced cohabitation, more independence, or modified commitment levels.

Gradual transition toward separation: Slowly increasing independence and emotional separation while maintaining care and respect for each other.

Clean break separation: Ending the relationship clearly and definitively when it becomes apparent that fundamental incompatibilities cannot be resolved.

The key is choosing consciously rather than drifting into decisions by default.

Quality of Life Assessment

Honest relationship evaluation requires examining how the relationship affects your overall life satisfaction and well-being.

Areas to assess:

Daily emotional experience: Do you feel generally happy, content, and emotionally nourished, or chronically stressed, lonely, and depleted?

Social connections: Are you able to maintain fulfilling friendships and family relationships, or has the romantic relationship consumed most of your emotional energy?

Personal growth and goals: Can you pursue your individual interests, career ambitions, and personal development, or are these sacrificed to relationship management?

Physical health: Is your physical well-being stable and positive, or are you experiencing stress-related health problems?

Future excitement: Do you feel enthusiastic about your life direction and future possibilities, or primarily worried about relationship dynamics?

Sense of self: Do you feel like yourself in this relationship, or have you lost touch with your identity and interests?

Red flag quality of life indicators:

Chronic stress that affects sleep, health, or daily functioning

Social isolation due to relationship demands or embarrassment

Career or educational sacrifices to accommodate relationship needs

Loss of individual identity or interests

Persistent depression, anxiety, or other mental health symptoms

Feeling trapped or hopeless about future possibilities

Physical health problems related to relationship stress

When relationship dynamics consistently undermine quality of life despite both people's efforts, fundamental changes become necessary.

A Real-World Decision Journey

Consider a teacher whose partner was an architect with quiet BPD. After three years together and eighteen months of actively working on quiet BPD dynamics, the teacher needed to honestly assess their relationship's future.

The positive changes were real but limited. The architect had learned to express basic emotions and could communicate needs more directly. They engaged in individual therapy and could discuss their patterns intellectually. The relationship had less conflict and more understanding.

However, the deeper emotional intimacy the teacher needed remained elusive. The architect still withdrew during stress, avoided deeper emotional conversations, and couldn't provide emotional support when the teacher was struggling. Physical affection felt dutiful rather than spontaneous, and future planning remained surface-level.

The teacher realized they were accommodating the relationship's limitations while hoping for changes that might never occur. They felt chronically lonely despite being in a partnership and found themselves seeking emotional connection through friendships rather than their romantic relationship.

The decision process involved several difficult realizations:

First, the architect was genuinely doing their best with their current emotional capacity. The limitations weren't due to lack of effort or care but to genuine constraints around emotional expression and intimacy.

Second, the teacher's needs for emotional connection were legitimate and important. Wanting emotional intimacy, spontaneous affection, and mutual emotional support wasn't unreasonable or demanding.

Third, love existed on both sides but wasn't sufficient to bridge the gap between what each person could offer and what the other needed.

The teacher ultimately chose to end the relationship, not out of anger or disappointment, but from recognition that both people deserved partnerships better matched to their emotional needs and capacities.

The separation was difficult but ultimately allowed both people to pursue relationships more compatible with their emotional styles and needs.

When Children Are Involved

Having children significantly complicates relationship decisions and requires additional considerations beyond individual satisfaction.

Factors specific to families:

Children's emotional well-being: How are relationship dynamics affecting the children's emotional development and sense of security?

Modeling healthy relationships: What are children learning about emotional intimacy, communication, and partnership from observing your relationship?

Stability versus authenticity: Balancing children's need for stability with their need to see authentic emotional connection modeled.

Co-parenting capacity: Considering both people's ability to maintain cooperative, supportive co-parenting relationships regardless of romantic relationship status.

Extended support systems: Evaluating what family and community support exist for children regardless of relationship decisions.

Professional guidance for family decisions:

Family therapy: Working with professionals who can assess relationship impact on children and family dynamics.

Individual therapy: Processing the complex emotions and decisions involved in relationship choices when children are affected.

Parenting coordination: Professional support for developing effective co-parenting relationships whether you stay together or separate.

Children's therapy: Support for children who are affected by family stress or relationship changes.

Decisions involving children require professional guidance and careful consideration of multiple factors beyond individual relationship satisfaction.

Financial and Practical Considerations

Relationship decisions often involve significant practical implications that need honest assessment.

Financial factors:

Economic interdependence: Housing, shared debts, joint assets, and financial obligations that complicate separation.

Individual financial capacity: Ability to maintain desired lifestyle independently or with modified arrangements.

Professional impacts: How relationship decisions might affect career stability, location flexibility, or professional development.

Insurance and benefits: Healthcare, life insurance, and other benefits tied to relationship status.

Long-term financial planning: Retirement savings, property ownership, and other long-term financial considerations.

Practical considerations:

Housing arrangements: Where each person would live and how living situations would change.

Pet custody and care: Responsibilities for shared pets and their well-being.

Social and family disruption: Impact on extended family relationships, mutual friendships, and community connections.

Geographic factors: Whether relationship decisions require relocation or significant lifestyle changes.

Timeline and logistics: Practical steps and timeframes for implementing relationship decisions.

While practical factors shouldn't override fundamental emotional needs, they deserve honest consideration in decision-making processes.

Alternative Relationship Structures

Sometimes traditional relationship expectations don't match what's possible or desired, creating opportunities for creative arrangements that better serve both people's needs.

Modified cohabitation: Living separately or with reduced shared living space while maintaining romantic connection.

Reduced relationship intensity: Maintaining partnership while both people pursue some emotional needs through other relationships or individual fulfillment.

Seasonal or periodic separation: Structured breaks that allow individual recharging while maintaining long-term commitment.

Defined relationship scope: Clearly agreeing on what the relationship will and won't provide emotionally, with both people finding fulfillment elsewhere for unmet needs.

Trial separations: Temporary separations to assess individual well-being and relationship value without permanent commitment to ending the relationship.

Parallel individual development: Maintaining relationship while both people focus primarily on individual growth and development.

These alternatives work when both people genuinely prefer modified arrangements rather than using them to avoid difficult decisions about relationship compatibility.

Making Peace with Difficult Decisions

Whether you choose to stay, leave, or redefine your relationship, finding peace with your decision requires accepting certain realities about love and compatibility.

Accepting relationship limitations:

Love doesn't automatically create compatibility: Two people can genuinely love each other while being fundamentally mismatched in emotional needs and capacity.

Good intentions don't guarantee good outcomes: Both people can be trying their best while still unable to create a satisfying relationship.

Some problems don't have solutions: Certain emotional limitations or incompatibilities might be permanent rather than temporary challenges to overcome.

Timing matters: Sometimes people are right for each other at the wrong time in their personal development.

Individual growth has limits: Not everyone can or will develop the emotional capacity needed for deep intimacy, regardless of effort or desire.

Finding peace with your choice:

Focus on what you learned: Every relationship teaches valuable lessons about yourself, your needs, and your capacity for love and growth.

Appreciate what was positive: Acknowledge the genuine love, care, and growth that occurred even if the relationship ultimately doesn't continue.

Trust your decision-making process: Recognize that you made the best choice possible with the information and emotional capacity you had at the time.

Allow grief for what wasn't possible: Mourning the relationship you hoped for while accepting the relationship that was actually possible.

Commit to your choice: Whatever you decide, invest fully rather than constantly questioning your decision.

Creating Your Decision Framework

Questions for honest self-assessment:

What are my non-negotiable emotional needs in a romantic relationship?

How well does this relationship meet those needs currently?

What changes would need to occur for me to feel satisfied long-term?

How likely are those changes based on patterns over the past year?

What would my life look like in five years if nothing significant changed in this relationship?

Am I staying out of love and satisfaction or out of fear, guilt, or hope for future change?

If I knew this relationship would remain exactly as it is now, would I choose to stay?

What advice would I give a friend in my exact situation?

Decision-making support:

Professional guidance: Working with therapists who can help you process complex emotions and decisions objectively.

Trusted advisors: Friends or family members who know you well and can provide honest perspective.

Written exploration: Journaling or written exercises that help clarify thoughts and feelings.

Trial periods: Testing different arrangements or separations to gather information about your needs and preferences.

Support groups: Connecting with others who have faced similar decisions.

The Path Forward

Whatever you decide about your relationship's future, the work you've done to understand quiet BPD and develop relationship skills will serve you well in all future relationships.

You've learned to distinguish between love and compatibility, support and enabling, patience and self-sacrifice. You've developed emotional awareness, communication skills, and boundary-setting abilities that will enhance any relationship you choose to build.

Most importantly, you've learned that loving someone doesn't require sacrificing your own emotional well-being, and that sometimes the most loving thing you can do is recognize when a relationship cannot provide what both people need to thrive.

Whether your future involves rebuilding this relationship with new understanding, creating an alternative arrangement that better serves both people's needs, or ending this relationship to pursue greater compatibility elsewhere, you have the tools and wisdom to make conscious, healthy choices about love and partnership.

The courage to make difficult decisions about relationships is also the courage to create the authentic, satisfying connections that make life meaningful and joyful.

Having examined these patterns through the lens of conscious choice-making, we arrive at understanding that every relationship decision - whether to stay, leave, or redefine - represents an opportunity for growth, wisdom, and deeper capacity for authentic love.

Appendix A: The Partner's Toolkit

The difference between surviving and thriving in a quiet BPD relationship often comes down to having the right words at the right moments. When your partner is shutting down emotionally, when you need to set a boundary without creating more distance, or when you're trying to validate their experience without losing yourself in the process - these are the moments when having practiced, effective language can transform difficult conversations into opportunities for connection.

This toolkit provides specific phrases, scripts, and frameworks that have proven helpful for partners navigating quiet BPD dynamics. These aren't magic formulas that will solve every problem, but they are tested approaches that can help you communicate more effectively while protecting your own emotional well-being.

Communication Scripts for Common Scenarios

When your partner says "I'm fine" but clearly isn't:

Instead of: "No, you're not fine. I can tell something's wrong." *Try:* "I hear you saying you're fine. I'm also noticing you seem quieter than usual. I'm here if that changes."

Instead of: "You're obviously upset about something." *Try:* "I believe you when you say you're fine. I also want you to know that if you're going through something, I care about how you're doing."

Instead of: "Why won't you tell me what's really wrong?" *Try:* "I respect that you might not want to talk about whatever you're experiencing. I also want you to know I'm available if that changes."

When your partner withdraws emotionally:

Instead of: "Why are you pulling away from me?" *Try:* "I notice you seem like you need some space right now. I'm here when you're ready to connect."

Instead of: "Did I do something wrong?" *Try:* "I can sense some distance between us. If there's something I can do differently, I'd like to know. If not, that's okay too."

Instead of: "We need to talk about this right now." *Try:* "I'd like to understand what's happening between us. When might be a good time to talk about it?"

When your partner minimizes their emotions:

Instead of: "This is obviously a big deal to you." *Try:* "Even if it doesn't feel like a big deal to you, I care about how you're experiencing it."

Instead of: "You shouldn't minimize your feelings." *Try:* "I appreciate you sharing this with me, regardless of how significant it feels to you."

Instead of: "Your emotions matter more than you think." *Try:* "What you're going through matters to me because you matter to me."

When you need to express your own emotional needs:

Instead of: "You never support me emotionally." *Try:* "I'm going through something difficult right now and could use some emotional support."

Instead of: "You're so emotionally unavailable." *Try:* "I need more emotional connection in our relationship. Can we talk about ways to create that?"

Instead of: "You don't care about my feelings." *Try:* "When I share my emotions, I need to feel heard and understood. That's really important to me."

143

When your partner takes excessive responsibility:

Instead of: "Stop blaming yourself for everything." *Try:* "I appreciate that you want to take responsibility. I also don't think this situation is entirely your responsibility."

Instead of: "You didn't cause this problem." *Try:* "There are multiple factors that contributed to this situation. You're one part of a bigger picture."

Instead of: "You need to stop being so hard on yourself." *Try:* "I see you being really tough on yourself right now. What would it be like to treat yourself with the same kindness you show others?"

Validation Phrase Library

Validation doesn't mean agreeing with everything your partner says or does. It means acknowledging their emotional experience as understandable and meaningful, even when you see things differently.

Basic validation phrases:

"That sounds really difficult." "I can understand why you'd feel that way." "That makes sense given what you're going through." "Anyone in your situation might feel similar." "Your feelings about this are completely valid." "I can see why this would be important to you." "That sounds overwhelming." "I believe you when you say this is hard."

Validation when you disagree:

"I can see why you'd see it that way, even though I might view it differently." "Your perspective makes sense from your experience." "I understand why this feels true for you right now." "Even though we see this differently, I can appreciate how you're experiencing it." "Your feelings about this are valid, even if we disagree about the facts."

Validation during emotional shutdown:

"I can see you're having a hard time right now." "It makes sense that you'd need some space to process this." "I understand that sharing emotions can feel difficult sometimes." "Your way of handling stress is understandable given your experience." "I can see you're doing the best you can right now."

Validation without fixing:

"That sounds really challenging. You don't have to figure it out right now." "I hear how difficult this is for you. You don't need to change how you're feeling." "This sounds like a lot to carry. I'm here with you in this." "I can see this is painful. You don't have to feel differently about it."

Validation during conflict:

"I can see you're feeling hurt by what I said." "It makes sense that you'd be upset about this." "I understand this conversation is difficult for both of us." "Your concerns about this situation are valid." "I can see we both care about this, even though we're approaching it differently."

Boundary-Setting Templates

Setting boundaries in quiet BPD relationships requires clear, kind language that protects your well-being without triggering abandonment fears.

Boundaries around emotional responsibility:

"I care about your emotional well-being, and I can't be responsible for managing your emotions."

"I want to support you through difficult times, and I also need you to take primary responsibility for your emotional regulation."

"I'm happy to provide comfort when you're struggling, and I can't be your only source of emotional support."

"I love you and want to help, and I also need you to develop your own emotional coping tools."

Boundaries around communication:

"I need you to communicate your needs directly rather than expecting me to guess what you need."

"I'm willing to have difficult conversations, and I need them to happen when we're both emotionally available."

"I want to understand how you're feeling, and I need you to use words rather than indirect signals."

"I care about your perspective, and I also need my own feelings and viewpoints to be heard and respected."

Boundaries around availability:

"I want to be here for you, and I also need some time and space for my own emotional needs."

"I'm committed to supporting you, and I also need to maintain my own friendships and interests."

"I love spending time together, and I also need some regular time for myself."

"I want to help during your difficult times, and I can't be available 24/7 for emotional crises."

Boundaries around problem-solving:

"I care about the problems you're facing, and I need you to take the lead in finding solutions."

"I'm happy to listen and offer support, and I can't fix your emotional struggles for you."

146

"I want to help when you ask for specific support, and I won't try to solve problems you haven't asked me to address."

"I believe in your ability to handle your challenges, with professional help when needed."

Gentle boundary enforcement:

"I mentioned that I need [specific boundary]. I'm still committed to that."

"This is bumping up against a boundary I've set. Can we try a different approach?"

"I love you and this conversation is crossing into territory that doesn't work for me."

"I need to take care of myself right now, which means [specific boundary action]."

Daily and Weekly Check-In Formats

Regular check-ins create opportunities for connection without the pressure of crisis-driven conversations.

Daily emotional weather report:

"How's your emotional energy today - high, medium, or low?" "What's one thing going well for you today?" "Is there anything you need from me today?" "What's your stress level like right now?" "How are you feeling about us today?"

Weekly relationship check-in:

Appreciation: "What's one thing you appreciated about our relationship this week?"

Concerns: "Is there anything about our relationship that's been on your mind?"

Needs: "What's one thing you need more of from me this week?"

Support: "How can I best support you in the coming week?"

Connection: "What's one way we could connect more this week?"

Monthly deeper check-in:

Individual growth: "How are you feeling about your personal growth lately?"

Relationship satisfaction: "What's working well for you in our relationship? What could be better?"

Future planning: "What are you looking forward to in our relationship?"

Challenges: "What's been most challenging for you lately, and how can I support you?"

Gratitude: "What are you most grateful for in your life right now?"

Crisis prevention check-in:

"On a scale of 1-10, how stable are you feeling emotionally?" "What are your stress levels like this week?" "Are there any situations coming up that might be challenging for you?" "What helps you feel most grounded and stable?" "Is there anything that would help prevent overwhelm this week?"

Crisis Intervention Protocols

Having a plan for crisis situations reduces anxiety and ensures both people know what to do when things become overwhelming.

Early warning signs checklist:

□ Partner seems more withdrawn than usual □ Changes in sleep or eating patterns □ Increased emotional numbness or disconnection □ Perfectionism or control behaviors escalating □ Mentions feeling "empty" or "numb" □ Avoiding activities they usually enjoy □ Increased self-criticism or guilt □ Physical symptoms of stress (headaches, tension) □ Difficulty concentrating or making decisions □ Expressing hopelessness about the future

Immediate crisis response steps:

1. **Stay calm:** Your emotional regulation helps create stability

2. **Assess safety:** Is there immediate risk of self-harm or suicide?

3. **Offer presence:** "I'm here with you. You're not alone."

4. **Avoid demanding explanations:** Don't ask "What's wrong?" repeatedly

5. **Provide practical support:** Handle immediate needs like food, comfort, safety

6. **Contact support if needed:** Use pre-arranged crisis contacts when appropriate

Crisis communication approaches:

"I can see you're really struggling right now." "You don't have to talk about it, but I want you to know I'm here." "What would help you feel safer right now?" "I care about you and I'm staying with you through this." "You don't have to handle this alone."

Professional help decision tree:

Call emergency services (911) if:

- Direct threats of suicide or self-harm

- Inability to ensure their own safety

- Severe dissociation or loss of contact with reality

- Dangerous behaviors that threaten immediate safety

Contact crisis hotline if:

- Thoughts of self-harm without immediate plan

- Severe depression or hopelessness

- Need for immediate professional guidance
- Overwhelm that exceeds your ability to support

Schedule urgent therapy if:

- Persistent crisis symptoms lasting several days
- Need for professional assessment
- Crisis patterns that are becoming frequent
- Request for increased professional support

Post-crisis recovery support:

"How are you feeling now that the intensity has passed?" "What helped most during the difficult time?" "Is there anything you need as you recover from this?" "What can we do differently if this happens again?" "I'm proud of you for getting through that difficult time."

Partner self-care during crisis:

□ Contact your own support person □ Practice emotional grounding techniques □ Take breaks when possible □ Maintain basic self-care (eating, sleeping) □ Limit crisis support to what you can sustainably provide □ Seek professional guidance if crisis becomes recurring pattern

Safety planning elements:

Warning signs specific to your partner Coping strategies that have worked before Support people who can be contacted Professional resources and contact information Environmental safety measures Agreements about when to involve others

Crisis supplies to keep available:

- Crisis hotline numbers
- Therapist emergency contact information
- Comfort items (blankets, tea, music)

- Grounding tools (ice cubes, strong scents, textured objects)

- Emergency medications if applicable

- Backup childcare contacts if needed

This toolkit becomes more effective with practice and personalization. Adapt these scripts and approaches to match your communication style and your partner's specific needs. The goal isn't perfect execution but rather having tools that help you respond thoughtfully rather than reactively during challenging moments.

Most importantly, these tools work best when combined with appropriate professional support, individual self-care, and realistic expectations about what partners can and cannot provide for each other's emotional well-being.

Appendix B: Professional Resources Directory

Finding appropriate professional help for quiet BPD requires knowing what to look for and where to find specialized providers who understand these presentations. This directory provides specific guidance for locating qualified professionals and accessing specialized programs designed for both individuals with quiet BPD and their partners.

RO-DBT Trained Therapist Locator Information

Radically Open Dialectical Behavior Therapy (RO-DBT) is specifically designed for overcontrolled personalities, making it particularly relevant for quiet BPD presentations.

Official RO-DBT Resources:

Radically Open Ltd. Official Website

- Provider directory for certified RO-DBT therapists

- Training programs and certification requirements

- Educational resources about overcontrol

- Contact: www.radicallyopen.net

RO-DBT Training Centers:

- Duke University (Durham, NC) - Original RO-DBT development site

- University of Southampton (UK) - European training center

- University of Nevada, Reno - Western US training hub

Finding RO-DBT Providers:

Questions to ask potential therapists: "Are you trained in RO-DBT or familiar with overcontrolled personality presentations?" "Do you have experience working with quiet or internalized BPD?" "How do you approach therapy with clients who have difficulty expressing emotions?" "What's your experience with people who appear high-functioning but struggle with internal emotional regulation?"

Alternative search terms to use:

- Overcontrolled personality disorder treatment
- Quiet borderline personality disorder therapy
- Internalized BPD treatment
- Emotional overcontrol therapy
- High-functioning BPD treatment

When RO-DBT isn't available:

Look for therapists with training in:

- Standard DBT who understand overcontrol
- Emotion-Focused Therapy (EFT)
- Schema Therapy
- Mentalization-Based Therapy (MBT)
- Attachment-based therapies

Couple's Therapy Programs for BPD

Specialized couple's therapy programs understand the unique dynamics of relationships involving BPD.

Emotionally Focused Therapy (EFT) for BPD:

International Centre for Excellence in EFT (ICEEFT)

- Certified EFT therapist directory

- Training programs for relationship therapy

- Specialized approaches for attachment disorders

- Contact: www.iceeft.com

EFT Externships and Training:

- Introductory training programs available nationwide

- Advanced training for complex presentations

- Supervision groups for ongoing skill development

Gottman Method Programs:

The Gottman Institute

- Therapist referral network

- Assessment tools for relationship dynamics

- Weekend intensives for couples

- Online resources and assessments

- Contact: www.gottman.com

DBT for Couples Programs:

Behavioral Tech (Linehan Institute)

- DBT couples therapy training

- Provider directory for DBT-trained therapists

- Specialized intensives for personality disorder relationships

- Contact: www.behavioraltech.org

Specialized BPD Couple Programs:

McLean Hospital (Boston, MA)

- Intensive couple's programs

- Family education and support
- Residential and outpatient options

Menninger Clinic (Houston, TX)

- Couple's therapy specializing in personality disorders
- Family systems approaches
- Intensive outpatient programs

Online Support Communities

Digital communities provide connection and support when local resources aren't available.

Moderated Professional Communities:

Psychology Today Support Groups

- Facilitator-led online groups
- BPD-specific partner support
- Regular meeting schedules
- Contact: www.psychologytoday.com/us/groups

BetterHelp Group Therapy

- Professional-led online groups
- Partner-specific support groups
- Flexible scheduling options
- Contact: www.betterhelp.com

Peer Support Communities:

Reddit Communities:

- r/BPDlovedones (115,000+ members)
- r/BPDPartners

- r/BPDsupport Guidelines: Focus on support rather than venting; avoid diagnosing; maintain anonymity

Facebook Support Groups:

- "Loving Someone with BPD"

- "BPD Family and Friends Support"

- "Partners of People with BPD" Guidelines: Private groups requiring approval; moderated discussions; respectful communication

Professional Organizations:

National Education Alliance for Borderline Personality Disorder (NEA-BPD)

- Family education programs

- Support group listings

- Educational webinars

- Annual conference

- Contact: www.borderlinepersonalitydisorder.org

National Alliance on Mental Illness (NAMI)

- Local support groups

- Family-to-family education programs

- Peer support training

- Crisis resources

- Contact: www.nami.org

Educational Programs

Structured educational programs provide comprehensive understanding of BPD dynamics and relationship strategies.

Family Connections Program:

National Education Alliance for BPD

- 12-week educational series
- Led by trained family members
- Evidence-based curriculum
- Available nationwide
- Free of charge
- Contact local NAMI chapters or NEA-BPD

Program Components:

- Understanding BPD symptoms and treatments
- Communication skills training
- Boundary setting and self-care
- Crisis management
- Supporting recovery
- Building family resilience

DBT Family Skills Groups:

Behavioral Tech Training

- Family member skills training
- Communication and validation techniques
- Emotion regulation for family members
- Crisis survival strategies
- Contact certified DBT providers

Online Educational Platforms:

Coursera Mental Health Courses

- "Understanding Mental Health" (Yale University)

- "De-Mystifying Mindfulness" (University of Virginia)

- "Managing Mental Health During COVID-19" (University of Toronto)

Udemy Relationship Courses

- "Healthy Relationships and Communication"

- "Boundaries in Relationships"

- "Understanding Personality Disorders"

Professional Training Opportunities:

Continuing Education for Mental Health

- BPD treatment training

- Family therapy certification

- Crisis intervention training

- Available for both professionals and educated family members

Recommended Books and Evidence-Based Resources

Essential Reading for Partners:

Foundational Understanding:

- "Stop Walking on Eggshells" by Paul Mason and Randi Kreger

- "The Essential Family Guide to Borderline Personality Disorder" by Randi Kreger

- "Loving Someone with Borderline Personality Disorder" by Shari Manning

Communication and Relationship Skills:

- "Hold Me Tight" by Sue Johnson (EFT approach)

- "The Seven Principles for Making Marriage Work" by John Gottman

- "Attached" by Amir Levine and Rachel Heller (attachment styles)

Self-Care and Boundary Setting:

- "Boundaries" by Henry Cloud and John Townsend

- "Self-Compassion" by Kristin Neff

- "The Gifts of Imperfection" by Brené Brown

Professional and Academic Resources:

Clinical Understanding:

- "Dialectical Behavior Therapy with Suicidal Adolescents" by Marsha Linehan

- "Borderline Personality Disorder: A Complete Guide to the Signs, Symptoms, and Treatment Options" by Jerold Kreisman

- "Treatment of Borderline Personality Disorder: A Guide to Evidence-Based Practice" by Joel Paris

Research and Theory:

- "Attachment in Psychotherapy" by David Wallin

- "The Body Keeps the Score" by Bessel van der Kolk

- "Radically Open Dialectical Behavior Therapy" by Thomas Lynch

Specialized Quiet BPD Resources:

Understanding Overcontrol:

- "Radically Open DBT" by Thomas Lynch

- "The Highly Sensitive Person" by Elaine Aron

- "Quiet: The Power of Introverts in a World That Can't Stop Talking" by Susan Cain

Assessment and Evaluation Tools

Professional assessment tools help identify quiet BPD presentations and track progress.

Self-Assessment Tools:

McLean Screening Instrument for BPD

- Brief screening questionnaire

- Available through mental health providers

- Helps identify potential BPD features

Overcontrol Questionnaire (OC-Q)

- Developed by Thomas Lynch for RO-DBT

- Assesses overcontrolled personality features

- Available through RO-DBT trained providers

Professional Assessment:

Structured Clinical Interview for DSM-5 Personality Disorders (SCID-5-PD)

- Comprehensive personality disorder assessment

- Administered by qualified mental health professionals

- Gold standard for personality disorder diagnosis

Borderline Personality Disorder Severity Index (BPDSI)

- Assesses severity of BPD symptoms

- Tracks treatment progress over time
- Used by specialized BPD treatment programs

Relationship Assessment:

Dyadic Adjustment Scale (DAS)

- Measures relationship satisfaction and adjustment
- Useful for couple's therapy planning
- Available through relationship therapists

Experiences in Close Relationships-Revised (ECR-R)

- Assesses attachment styles in relationships
- Helps understand relationship dynamics
- Available through attachment-informed therapists

Insurance and Financial Resources

Insurance Navigation:

Mental Health Parity Information:

- Know your rights under mental health parity laws
- Insurance companies must provide equal coverage for mental health
- Appeals processes for denied claims
- Contact your state insurance commissioner for disputes

Medicare/Medicaid Resources:

- Coverage for mental health services
- Provider directories for covered therapists
- Appeals processes for coverage decisions

Financial Assistance:

Sliding Scale Providers:

- Community mental health centers
- Graduate training programs
- Private practice therapists offering reduced fees
- Religious or community organizations

Grant and Scholarship Programs:

- NAMI local affiliates sometimes offer treatment scholarships
- University training programs often provide low-cost services
- Employee assistance programs through employers

Treatment Cost Planning:

Typical Costs (varies by region):

- Individual therapy: $100-300 per session
- Couple's therapy: $150-400 per session
- Intensive programs: $200-500 per day
- Psychiatric evaluation: $300-800 initial, $100-200 follow-up

Insurance Maximization Strategies:

- Use in-network providers when possible
- Understand your annual deductible and out-of-pocket maximum
- Keep detailed records of all mental health expenses
- Consider Health Savings Account (HSA) for eligible expenses

This directory serves as a starting point for finding appropriate professional support. Always verify credentials, training, and specialization when selecting mental health providers. The most important factor is finding professionals who understand quiet BPD presentations and can provide effective, compassionate care for both individuals and relationships.

Appendix C: Emergency Planning Documents

Crisis situations require immediate access to clear information and predetermined plans. When someone is experiencing internal emotional crisis, there's no time to research phone numbers, figure out insurance coverage, or debate who to call for help. This appendix provides templates and resources you can prepare in advance and access quickly during emergency situations.

Safety Plan Templates

A comprehensive safety plan addresses both immediate crisis response and longer-term safety management.

Personal Safety Plan for Partner with Quiet BPD

Warning Signs I Notice: □ Early signs (fatigue, withdrawal, perfectionism increase) □ Medium signs (emotional numbness, self-criticism, isolation) □ Late signs (hopelessness, mentions of being a burden, research into self-harm)

Internal Coping Strategies I Can Try: □ Deep breathing exercises □ Cold water on face/hands □ Physical grounding (feet on floor, hands on solid surface) □ Listening to specific calming music □ Looking at photos that bring comfort □ Reading predetermined comforting texts or quotes

Social Contacts Who Can Help:

1. Primary support person: _____ Phone: _____ Available when: _____

2. Secondary support: _____ Phone: _____ Available when: _____

3. Crisis hotline: 988 (24/7 mental health crisis line)

4. Emergency contact: _____ Phone: _____ Relationship: _____

Professional Support:

- Therapist: _____ Phone: _____

- Psychiatrist: _____ Phone: _____

- Primary doctor: _____ Phone: _____

- Preferred hospital: _____ Address: _____

Environmental Safety:

□ Remove or secure potentially harmful items

□ Create calming environment (lighting, temperature, music)

□ Have comfort items easily accessible

□ Ensure safe transportation if needed

Reasons for Living/Recovery Motivation:

1. _____
2. _____
3. _____
4. _____
5. _____

Partner Support Safety Plan

How I Know My Partner Is in Crisis: □ Behavioral changes I observe □ Emotional atmosphere shifts I sense □ Physical signs I notice □ Communication pattern changes

Immediate Response Steps:

1. Stay calm and grounded myself

2. Assess immediate safety concerns

3. Use validation phrases from toolkit

4. Offer specific support without overwhelming

5. Contact professional help if needed

My Support During Crisis:

- My primary support person: _____

- My therapist: _____

- My crisis support: _____

- Self-care practices I can do quickly: _____

Boundaries During Crisis:

☐ What I can realistically provide

☐ What I need to refer to professionals

☐ How long I can sustain crisis support

☐ When I need to involve others

Crisis Contact Wallet Cards

Create wallet-sized cards with essential crisis information for immediate access.

Card 1: Emergency Contacts

CRISIS CONTACTS

National Crisis Line: 988

Text Crisis Line: Text HOME to 741741

Emergency Services: 911

Therapist: _____

Phone: _____

After-hours: _____

Psychiatrist: _____

Phone: _____

Emergency: _____

Primary Support Person: _____

Phone: _____

Insurance Group #: _____

Policy #: _____

Card 2: Medical Information

MEDICAL INFORMATION

Name: _____

DOB: _____

Allergies: _____

Current Medications:

_____

_____

_____

Medical Conditions:

_____

_____

Emergency Contact: _____

Phone: _____

Card 3: Crisis Response Guide

CRISIS RESPONSE REMINDERS

If Suicidal Thoughts:

- Call 988 immediately

- Don't leave alone

- Remove harmful items

- Go to nearest ER

If Severe Anxiety/Panic:

- Ground with 5-4-3-2-1 technique

- Cold water on face

- Call support person

- Use breathing exercises

If Dissociation:

- Name current location aloud

- Touch solid objects

- Call someone you trust

- Avoid driving

Card 4: Hospital Information

PREFERRED HOSPITALS

Primary Choice: _____

Address: _____

Phone: _____

Secondary Choice: _____

Address: _____

Phone: _____

Insurance Accepted: _____

Primary Doctor: _____

Pharmacy: _____

Address: _____

Phone: _____

Medication Management Protocols

For partners taking psychiatric medications, organized medication management becomes crucial during crisis periods.

Daily Medication Tracker

Current Medications:

Medication: _____ Dose: _____ Time: _____
Purpose: _____

Medication: _____ Dose: _____ Time: _____
Purpose: _____

Medication: _____ Dose: _____ Time: _____
Purpose: _____

Weekly Pill Organization:

□ Use pill organizer with day/time compartments

□ Fill weekly on same day each week

□ Check for running low on medications

□ Note any side effects or concerns

Medication Emergency Kit:

□ 3-day supply of all medications in separate container

□ List of all medications with doses and prescribing doctors

□ Pharmacy contact information

□ Insurance card copy

□ Allergy information

Medication Crisis Protocols:

If Medications Are Missed:

1. Check how long since last dose

2. Consult medication instruction sheet

3. Call pharmacist for guidance if uncertain

4. Contact prescribing doctor if multiple doses missed

5. Monitor for withdrawal symptoms

If Side Effects Occur:

1. Document specific symptoms and timing

2. Check medication information for known side effects

3. Contact prescribing doctor for guidance

4. Call emergency services if severe reactions (difficulty breathing, chest pain, severe allergic reactions)

Medication Management During Crisis:

□ Partner may need help remembering to take medications

□ Monitor for medication compliance during emotional distress

□ Contact psychiatrist if crisis might require medication adjustments
□ Keep accurate records of any missed doses

Legal Consideration Checklists

Understanding legal rights and options becomes important during crisis situations.

Advanced Directive Preparation

Mental Health Advance Directive: □ Preferred treatment approaches during crisis □ Medications to avoid or prefer □ Preferred hospitals or treatment facilities □ People authorized to make decisions if unable □ Specific treatment wishes or limitations

Power of Attorney Considerations: □ Healthcare power of attorney designation □ Financial power of attorney if needed □ Clear instructions about when powers activate □ Copies provided to all relevant parties

Crisis Intervention Rights

Voluntary Hospitalization: □ Right to admit yourself to psychiatric facility □ Right to participate in treatment planning □ Right to refuse certain treatments □ Right to have advocate or support person involved

Involuntary Hold Procedures: □ Criteria for involuntary psychiatric hold (varies by state) □ Time limits for evaluation and treatment □ Rights during involuntary treatment □ Appeal processes and legal representation

Patient Rights During Crisis:

□ Right to informed consent for treatment

□ Right to confidentiality and privacy

□ Right to have cultural and religious preferences respected

□ Right to have family/friends involved in treatment planning (with permission)

Legal Documentation Checklist

□ Health insurance cards and information

⊓ Government-issued identification

□ Emergency contact information

□ Medical power of attorney documents

□ Mental health advance directive

□ List of current medications and allergies

□ Primary care physician information

□ Preferred hospital information

□ Insurance pre-authorization information if required

Insurance Navigation Guide

Understanding insurance coverage before crisis situations helps ensure appropriate care access.

Pre-Crisis Insurance Verification

Coverage Information to Verify: □ Mental health coverage limits (sessions per year, lifetime limits) □ Emergency room coverage for psychiatric emergencies □ Inpatient psychiatric coverage and time limits □ Out-of-network coverage for mental health providers □ Pre-authorization requirements for psychiatric treatment

Provider Network Information: □ List of in-network psychiatrists and therapists □ In-network hospitals with psychiatric units □ Crisis intervention services covered □ Intensive outpatient programs available

Coverage Limitations to Understand: □ Annual deductible amounts for mental health □ Co-payment amounts for different types of services □ Co-insurance percentages for mental health treatment □ Out-of-pocket maximum for mental health services

Crisis Situation Insurance Protocols

Emergency Room Visits: □ Most insurance plans cover psychiatric emergencies □ Bring insurance card and identification □ Request social worker to help with insurance issues □ Get copies of all treatment records for insurance claims

Psychiatric Hospitalization: □ Insurance typically covers medically necessary psychiatric hospitalization □ Hospital will usually verify coverage upon admission □ Request case manager to help coordinate discharge planning □ Understand coverage limits for length of stay

Following Up on Claims: □ Keep detailed records of all services received □ Follow up on insurance claims within 30 days □ Appeal denied claims if treatment was medically necessary □ Use insurance company's mental health advocacy services

Financial Protection Strategies

Documentation for Insurance: □ Keep copies of all mental health treatment records □ Save receipts for all mental health-related expenses □ Document how treatment relates to medical necessity □ Keep records of time off work due to mental health treatment

Appeal Processes: □ Understand your insurance plan's appeal process □ Know time limits for filing appeals □ Get written denials to appeal properly □ Use your state's insurance commissioner as resource for appeals

Alternative Funding Sources: □ Employee assistance programs through work □ Community mental health center sliding scale fees □ University training programs with reduced-cost services □ Religious or community organization assistance programs

Emergency Contact Quick Reference

Immediate Crisis:

- Emergency Services: 911
- National Crisis Line: 988
- Crisis Text Line: Text HOME to 741741

Professional Support:

- Therapist: _____
- Psychiatrist: _____
- Primary Care Doctor: _____

Personal Support:

- Primary Support Person: _____
- Secondary Support: _____

174

- Family Emergency Contact: _____

Medical Information:

- Insurance Company: _____

- Policy Number: _____

- Preferred Hospital: _____

This emergency planning ensures that during crisis situations, you have immediate access to the information and resources needed to provide appropriate support and access professional help quickly and effectively.

Appendix D: Success Stories and Case Studies

Real transformation in quiet BPD relationships is possible, but it often looks different from dramatic breakthrough moments portrayed in movies or books. Change tends to be gradual, sometimes invisible to outside observers, and requires sustained commitment from both people over months or years. These stories illustrate what genuine progress looks like and how couples navigate the challenges of building authentic intimacy when one person has learned to hide their emotional experience.

Five Detailed Couple Journeys

Journey One: The Gradual Opening

A nurse and a software developer had been together for four years when they first learned about quiet BPD. The developer had always been emotionally reserved, which initially attracted the nurse who had grown up in a chaotic household and appreciated the developer's calm stability.

Over time, however, the nurse began feeling lonely despite being in a committed relationship. The developer provided practical support and was reliably present, but conversations never went deeper than daily logistics and surface topics. When the nurse tried to share emotions or concerns, the developer would listen politely but offer only practical solutions or would suggest the nurse talk to friends about emotional needs.

The turning point came during a family crisis when the nurse's parent was hospitalized. Despite this being an obviously stressful situation, the developer seemed confused about why the nurse needed emotional support beyond the practical help they were already providing (handling household tasks, arranging time off work, managing logistics).

After learning about quiet BPD, both people began understanding their dynamic differently. The developer realized they had learned in childhood that emotional expression led to criticism, so they'd developed skills for hiding feelings so effectively that even they couldn't access them easily.

The change process took nearly two years and involved several key developments:

Individual work: The developer began therapy specifically focused on emotional awareness and expression. They started with basic exercises like identifying physical sensations and connecting them to possible emotions.

Gradual emotional sharing: Instead of expecting deep emotional conversations, they started with the developer sharing simple feeling observations: "I felt frustrated with that traffic jam" or "I enjoyed that movie more than I expected."

Validation without pursuit: The nurse learned to acknowledge the developer's small emotional offerings without immediately asking for more: "Thanks for sharing that with me" instead of "Tell me more about how you felt."

Crisis support modification: During stressful periods, instead of expecting the developer to provide emotional comfort, the nurse would ask for specific practical support while seeking emotional support from friends or family.

Patience with setbacks: Progress wasn't linear. The developer would sometimes shut down during stressful periods or revert to emotional unavailability during conflicts.

After two years, their relationship looked different but not dramatically transformed. The developer could share basic emotions and occasionally provided comfort during the nurse's difficult times.

They could discuss future plans and express appreciation for their relationship. While deep emotional intimacy remained limited, both people felt more connected and understood.

The nurse learned to appreciate the developer's unique way of showing care (through actions rather than words) while maintaining friendships that provided emotional reciprocity. The developer learned that sharing emotions actually strengthened their relationship rather than creating the rejection they'd always feared.

Journey Two: The Recovery Partnership

A teacher and an accountant met during the accountant's recovery from a severe depression that had led to their first experience with therapy. The accountant had been diagnosed with BPD during hospitalization but had learned significant emotional regulation skills through intensive treatment.

However, as the accountant's crisis symptoms improved, the teacher began noticing quiet BPD patterns that the crisis-focused treatment hadn't addressed. The accountant rarely shared emotions spontaneously, avoided conflict completely, and became overwhelmed by the teacher's emotional expression despite having learned crisis management skills.

Their approach to quiet BPD was different because both people understood from the beginning that ongoing professional support would be necessary. They treated emotional development as a joint project rather than something the accountant needed to "fix" individually.

Couple's therapy focus: They worked with a therapist trained in both DBT and EFT who could address both the accountant's emotional avoidance and their attachment dynamics as a couple.

Structured emotional practice: They developed formal practices for emotional sharing, starting with scheduled 10-minute check-ins where each person shared one emotion from their day.

Conflict resolution protocols: Since the accountant tended to shut down during disagreements, they developed structured approaches to conflict that provided safety and predictability.

Individual growth support: The teacher also engaged in individual therapy to process their own patterns and needs rather than focusing exclusively on the accountant's growth.

Professional crisis management: They developed clear agreements about when to involve the accountant's therapist or psychiatrist, taking pressure off the teacher to manage all emotional situations.

The transformation happened over three years and included both significant progress and ongoing limitations. The accountant developed capacity for emotional intimacy that surpassed what either person had thought possible, but they still needed more structure and support than typical relationships require.

Their success came from accepting that their relationship would always require more conscious effort and professional support than other relationships while celebrating the genuine intimacy they were able to create within those parameters.

Journey Three: The Redefinition Success

A physical therapist and a graphic designer had been married for eight years with two young children when they first addressed quiet BPD dynamics. The designer had always been the "easy" partner - never demanding, rarely upset, excellent with children and household management. But the physical therapist felt increasingly lonely and began questioning whether they were compatible long-term.

Instead of ending their marriage, they chose to redefine their relationship structure to better accommodate both people's needs and limitations.

Modified expectations: They agreed that their marriage would provide companionship, co-parenting partnership, and practical support, while the physical therapist would seek emotional intimacy through friendships and individual pursuits.

Structured emotional connection: The designer committed to specific emotional sharing practices (weekly appreciation, monthly relationship check-ins) that felt manageable rather than overwhelming.

Individual fulfillment priority: Both people focused on developing their individual interests and friendships rather than expecting the marriage to meet all emotional needs.

Professional co-parenting: They worked with a family therapist to ensure their modified relationship structure supported healthy child development.

Periodic reassessment: They agreed to annually evaluate whether their arrangement was working for both people and their children.

This approach worked because both people genuinely preferred their modified arrangement to either ending the marriage or struggling with traditional emotional intimacy expectations. The physical therapist found fulfilling emotional connections through friendships while appreciating the designer's reliability and partnership. The designer felt relieved from pressure to provide emotional intimacy they couldn't sustain while contributing meaningfully to the partnership.

After five years with this arrangement, both people reported higher relationship satisfaction than they'd experienced when trying to force traditional emotional intimacy.

Journey Four: The Later-Life Learning

A retired teacher and a retired engineer had been married for thirty-five years when their adult children pointed out concerning patterns in their relationship. The engineer had always been emotionally distant, which the teacher had attributed to generational and gender differences. However, their children noticed that family gatherings always revolved around avoiding any topic that might upset the engineer, while the teacher managed all emotional aspects of family relationships.

Learning about quiet BPD in their sixties brought both relief and challenge. Relief because patterns that had confused them for decades finally made sense. Challenge because changing relationship dynamics after thirty-five years felt overwhelming.

Gentle exploration: Instead of intensive therapy, they worked with a counselor who specialized in later-life relationships to explore their patterns without pressure for dramatic change.

Gradual boundary adjustment: The teacher slowly reduced their emotional management of family situations while the engineer gradually took more responsibility for family emotional needs.

Legacy consideration: They focused on how they wanted to model relationships for their grandchildren rather than trying to meet all their own unmet emotional needs.

Acceptance with growth: They accepted that major personality changes weren't realistic at their age while still creating more emotional balance in their relationship.

Family system involvement: They included their adult children in some discussions about changing family emotional dynamics.

The changes were modest but meaningful. The engineer learned to ask family members how they were feeling and to express appreciation directly. The teacher learned to let other family members handle their own emotional needs rather than managing everyone's feelings.

While deep emotional intimacy never developed, both people felt more authentic and balanced in their relationship. Their adult children noticed reduced family tension and more genuine interactions during family gatherings.

Journey Five: The Young Adult Success

A college student and a recent graduate began dating when both were in their early twenties. The graduate had grown up in a family where emotional expression was discouraged and had developed quiet BPD patterns as protection against criticism and rejection.

Their advantage was learning about these dynamics early in their relationship before problematic patterns became entrenched. They approached quiet BPD as information to understand rather than problems to solve.

Educational approach: Both people read about attachment styles, emotional development, and relationship skills rather than focusing exclusively on BPD pathology.

Professional guidance: They worked with a counselor during their first year together to develop healthy communication patterns from the beginning.

Friend and family involvement: They were open with friends and family about their learning process, creating support networks that understood their dynamics.

Individual development priority: Both people focused heavily on individual growth and career development while building their relationship skills.

Long-term perspective: They made decisions based on long-term compatibility rather than short-term emotional intensity.

Their relationship developed differently from typical young adult relationships. Instead of the intense emotional highs and lows common in early relationships, they built steady emotional intimacy gradually over time.

After four years together, they had developed communication skills and emotional intimacy that many couples take decades to achieve. The graduate had learned to recognize and express emotions appropriately, while the college student had developed skills for supporting emotional growth without managing their partner's emotions.

Their success came from approaching relationship skills as learnable abilities rather than assuming that healthy relationships happen naturally without conscious effort.

Partner Recovery Narratives

From Caretaker to Partner

A social worker had spent three years gradually becoming their partner's primary emotional support system without realizing it was happening. They monitored moods, anticipated needs, and took responsibility for preventing emotional crises while their partner remained passive in their own emotional life.

The recovery process involved:

Recognition: Realizing they had been doing their partner's emotional work while neglecting their own needs and growth.

Boundary development: Learning to distinguish between appropriate support and emotional caretaking.

Identity reclamation: Reconnecting with friends, interests, and goals that existed outside the relationship.

Professional support: Individual therapy focused on codependency patterns and self-care.

Gradual redistribution: Slowly returning emotional responsibility to their partner while maintaining appropriate support.

The transformation took eighteen months and involved significant relationship tension as their partner learned to take responsibility for emotional needs they'd been avoiding. However, the result was a more balanced partnership where both people participated actively in emotional support and relationship maintenance.

From Walking on Eggshells to Authentic Communication

A marketing professional had developed hypervigilance around their partner's emotional state, constantly monitoring for signs of withdrawal or distress. They had learned to communicate in careful, indirect ways to avoid triggering emotional shutdown.

Recovery involved:

Emotional boundary setting: Learning to distinguish between their own anxiety and their partner's emotional state.

Direct communication practice: Gradually returning to authentic expression of thoughts and feelings rather than managed communication.

Trigger acceptance: Understanding that their authentic expression might sometimes trigger their partner's withdrawal while maintaining appropriate boundaries.

Support system development: Building friendships where they could be completely authentic without emotional management.

Stress management: Developing techniques for managing their own anxiety rather than controlling their partner's emotions.

After one year of focused work, they had returned to authentic communication while maintaining sensitivity to their partner's emotional needs. The relationship became more genuine as both people could be themselves rather than managing each other's emotional experience.

Treatment Success Indicators

Recognizing genuine progress in quiet BPD relationships requires understanding what realistic improvement looks like.

Individual Progress for Partner with Quiet BPD:

Emotional awareness development:

- Can identify basic emotions (happy, sad, angry, anxious) in themselves

- Notices physical sensations that accompany emotions
- Recognizes emotional triggers and patterns
- Can distinguish between different types of emotional experiences

Communication improvements:

- Shares emotions directly rather than expecting partner to guess
- Can express needs and preferences clearly
- Asks for specific support when struggling
- Responds to partner's emotional expressions appropriately

Relationship engagement:

- Participates actively in conflict resolution rather than shutting down
- Shows interest in partner's emotional experience
- Takes initiative in emotional connection occasionally
- Can provide comfort and support when partner is struggling

Crisis management:

- Recognizes early warning signs of emotional overwhelm
- Uses coping strategies before reaching crisis level
- Communicates when professional help is needed
- Participates actively in safety planning

Partner Progress Indicators:

Boundary maintenance:

- Distinguishes between own emotions and partner's emotions

- Provides support without taking responsibility for partner's emotional regulation

- Maintains individual interests and friendships

- Sets limits on emotional labor without guilt

Communication skills:

- Expresses needs directly rather than expecting mind-reading

- Validates partner's emotions without immediately trying to fix them

- Responds to withdrawal without taking it personally

- Asks for what they need rather than hoping partner will notice

Self-care consistency:

- Maintains physical and emotional health regardless of relationship stress

- Seeks professional support when needed

- Has support systems outside the relationship

- Pursues individual goals and interests

Realistic expectations:

- Understands quiet BPD limitations without enabling avoidance

- Appreciates progress while maintaining appropriate relationship standards

- Makes decisions based on current reality rather than hoped-for changes

- Balances patience with self-protection

Relationship Transformation Examples

Transformation in Conflict Resolution

Before understanding quiet BPD: Disagreements would trigger the partner with quiet BPD to shut down emotionally, leaving the other partner to either drop the issue or fight alone. Conflicts never reached resolution and created increasing resentment.

After intervention: The couple developed structured approaches to conflict that accommodated emotional overwhelm while ensuring problems got addressed. They used written communication during difficult topics, took breaks when needed, and involved their therapist for particularly challenging issues.

Result: While conflicts still triggered some emotional withdrawal, they developed systems for working through problems together. Both people felt heard and conflicts reached actual resolution rather than being avoided or abandoned.

Transformation in Emotional Support

Before understanding: When the supporting partner experienced stress or difficulties, the partner with quiet BPD would offer practical help but seemed confused by requests for emotional comfort. The supporting partner learned to seek emotional support elsewhere while feeling rejected by their partner.

After intervention: The partner with quiet BPD learned specific ways to provide emotional support even when they couldn't access their own emotions easily. They developed scripts for validation and comfort that felt genuine rather than performed.

Result: While emotional support remained more structured than in typical relationships, both people felt that emotional needs were acknowledged and addressed rather than ignored or minimized.

Transformation in Crisis Management

Before understanding: Crises would involve the supporting partner trying to guess what was wrong while the partner with quiet BPD insisted they were fine. This created anxiety and helplessness for both people during difficult periods.

After intervention: They developed clear crisis protocols that included early warning sign recognition, communication strategies that felt safe for both people, and predetermined professional support contacts.

Result: While crises still occurred, both people knew how to respond effectively. The partner with quiet BPD felt supported rather than overwhelmed, while the supporting partner felt useful rather than helpless.

These success stories illustrate that transformation in quiet BPD relationships is possible but often requires patience, professional support, and willingness to create relationship structures that work for both people rather than forcing traditional relationship expectations onto unique dynamics.

The common thread across all successful couples was acceptance of limitations combined with commitment to growth within those limitations, realistic expectations paired with genuine effort, and professional support when needed rather than attempting to resolve complex dynamics through willpower alone.

References

Carpenter, R. W., & Trull, T. J. (2013). Components of emotion dysregulation in borderline personality disorder. *Current Psychiatry Reports, 15*(1), 335.

Chapman, A. L., & Gratz, K. L. (2007). *The borderline personality disorder survival guide*. New Harbinger Publications.

Chapman, A. L., & Gratz, K. L. (2019). Borderline personality disorder and emotion dysregulation. *Development and Psychopathology, 31*(3), 1143–1156.

Gottman, J. M., & Levenson, R. W. (2000). The timing of divorce: Predicting when a couple will divorce over a 14-year period. *Journal of Marriage and Family, 62*(3), 737–745.

Gratz, K. L., & Roemer, L. (2004). Multidimensional assessment of emotion regulation and dysregulation. *Journal of Psychopathology and Behavioral Assessment, 26*(1), 41–54.

Johnson, S. M. (2019). *Attachment theory in practice: Emotionally focused therapy (EFT) with individuals, couples, and families*. Guilford Press.

Kreisman, J. J., & Straus, H. (2004). *Sometimes I act crazy: Living with borderline personality disorder*. John Wiley & Sons.

Linehan, M. M. (2014). *DBT skills training manual* (2nd ed.). Guilford Press.

Lynch, T. R. (2018). *Radically open dialectical behavior therapy: Theory and practice for treating disorders of overcontrol*. New Harbinger Publications.

Lynch, T. R., & Cheavens, J. S. (2008). Dialectical behavior therapy for comorbid personality disorders. *Journal of Clinical Psychology, 64*(2), 154–167.

Lynch, T. R., & Cuper, P. F. (2012). Dialectical behavior therapy of borderline and other personality disorders. In T. A. Widiger (Ed.), *The Oxford handbook of personality disorders* (pp. 785–793). Oxford University Press.

Lynch, T. R., Hempel, R. J., & Dunkley, C. (2015). Radically open-dialectical behavior therapy for disorders of over-control: Signaling matters. *American Journal of Psychotherapy, 69*(2), 141–162.

Miller, W. R., & Rollnick, S. (2012). *Motivational interviewing: Helping people change* (3rd ed.). Guilford Press.

Paris, J. (2020). *Treatment of borderline personality disorder: A guide to evidence-based practice* (2nd ed.). Guilford Press.

Prochaska, J. O., & DiClemente, C. C. (1983). Stages and processes of self-change of smoking. *Journal of Consulting and Clinical Psychology, 51*(3), 390–395.

Salsman, N. L., & Linehan, M. M. (2012). An investigation of the relationships among negative affect, difficulties in emotion regulation, and features of borderline personality disorder. *Journal of Psychopathology and Behavioral Assessment, 34*(2), 260–267.

Stanley, B., & Brown, G. K. (2012). Safety planning intervention: A brief intervention to mitigate suicide risk. *Cognitive and Behavioral Practice, 19*(2), 256–264.

Stiglmayr, C., Stecher-Mohr, J., Wagner, T., Meißner, J., Spretz, D., Steffens, C., ... & Roepke, S. (2014). Effectiveness of dialectical behavior therapy in routine outpatient care: The Berlin borderline study. *Borderline Personality Disorder and Emotion Dysregulation, 1*(20).

Stosny, S. (2013). *Living and loving after betrayal: How to heal from emotional abuse, deceit, infidelity, and chronic resentment.* New Harbinger Publications.

www.ingramcontent.com/pod-product-compliance
Lightning Source LLC
Chambersburg PA
CBHW072141270326
41931CB00010B/1835